The Gay Gospel

*A Survival Guide for
Gay 20Somethings
in America Today*

Justin Luke Zirilli

Extra Special Thanks

The book you are holding would not have been possible without the help of over 70 people who helped to raise the funds to publish it on Kickstarter. The following people went above and beyond giving extraordinarily generous amounts of money to make The Gay Gospel a reality. I owe them many, many thanks.

Super-Special Thanks goes to the following individuals: Jay Kuo, James Cook, Josh Bendat, Thomas Lyons, Marc Rayner, Jennifer Dotson, Mike Van Dyke, Robert Beleson, Rich Reilly, Chris Mix, Brendan Franklin, Colby J. Duhon, Gregory Dyrsten, Matt John, Anthony Luzzi, Chad Ryan, Jesse "Shameless" Gilday, Lorenzo Thione, DJ Toomuch Twoface, and Sean Donegan.

For Boyfriend Joe:
Always and Forever.

Contents

Extra Special Thanks	2
Introduction	3
The Book of Looking	5
You Don't NEED A Boyfriend	7
You're Not Even LOOKING For a Boyfriend!	10
Go After What You Want	13
The Art of Rejection	15
Ten Reasons You'll Be Rejected	18
Someone For Everyone	22
Be Bold; Be You	24
Hardcore Text	26
Ten Reasons NOT to Go Home with That Guy	29
We're ALL Fucked Up	33
The Ultimate Pick-Up Line	34
Going Home with a Straight Guy	37
The Spinning Wheels of Gay Dating	40
Game Over	43
To Catch a Catfish	45
The Book of Dating	49
The First Date	51
Keep It Positive	54
Find His Flaws... Fast	56
(Not) Going the Distance	58
How To Melt A Guy's Heart with $2	61
Slow Down!	64
He's Definitely Not into You	67
Eyes on Me!	70
Title Treatment	73
The Book of Loving	77
The Cinderella Phase	79
Moving In	82

How To Live Together	84
The Come Down	87
You Gotta Fight	89
An Open (or) Shut Case	91
Abuse is Never Okay	94
The Book of Breaking Up	**97**
When It's (Possibly) Time to Break Up	98
How To Break Up	102
How to Get Dumped	105
How to Get Over Him	108
The Book of Doing It	**111**
Safe Vs. Stupid	112
Gay Sex 101	114
Top Tactics	117
Best Bottom Behavior	121
One Night Only	124
Friends with Benefits (or Detriments)	127
Three, Four, or More	130
Face Your Fetishes	134
The Book of Partying	**137**
Finding the Balance	138
Doing Drugs	140
6 Ways to NOT Be A Drunken Mess	142
It's Never Too Late to Irish Exit	146
Party Pack Mentality	148
The Top 10 Things NOT To Do at The Gay Club	151
The Book of Living	**155**
Come Out, Come Out	156
Do Something	159
Work Hard, Dream Hard	162
Play For Karma	164
Avoid Unnecessary Conflict	165
Five Ways to Avoid Drama	167
Money Really Matters	171
All in the Family	175
Judge Not	177
Conclusion	**179**
Afterword	**180**
Special Thanks	**182**
About the Author	**183**

Foreword

By Michael Musto

It's hard enough to be human let alone gay and in your 20s, and when I found myself in that very situation some (mutter, mumble, cough) years ago I wished there had been a Justin Luke guidebook around to tell me how to pull it off. At twenty I was quite successfully graduating from Columbia College, but I didn't know what to do about it! I wanted to be a writer, but there was no journalism undergrad major offered in my college. Thus I had to major in English literature reading Jane Austen novels as if that had anything to do with the gossip and theater reviews I so desperately wanted to indulge in. Fortunately I had already done pieces not only for the school papers but for outside publications, so I had my foot in the door of what I considered big-time writing. And having sat in on some of the Columbia Journalism classes full of pretend press conferences and pseudo news coverage, I knew that continuing my education would be a complete waste of time and money. The real world awaited.

But what to do? Well I kept my freelancing going and eventually landed a job at Ideal, a sleazy company that put out monthly rags with misleading celebrity headlines full of quote marks within quotation marks. ("Cher 'Leaves' Sonny!" generally meant she left him to go shopping for an hour). I was the managing editor of one of those publications as well as a soap opera magazine immersing myself in daytime dramatics I didn't care about and celebrity goings-on that weren't even true. But I had a job! And I was young! And I had no earthly idea what I was doing!

Meanwhile I was so sexually inexperienced that when I went out with a male officemate and we ended up kissing, he criticized me for the frozen way I kept my head steady as if I were a puckered-up mannequin. I had a lot to learn, but with no guidebook I had to learn the hard way—on my own with a considerable amount of help from friends and compatriots. Fortunately, the LGBT community is an even better learning experience than graduate school. They'll teach you, guide you, show you things, and (like my officemate) read you very loudly when you're doing things wrong.

When it comes to nightlife, things are even more educational and I truly started at the top of the academic heap. One of my first clubs was the legendary '70s disco Studio 54, where all genders and sexualities merged under the glitterdome; everyone spent but somehow wiser by the end of the night (when the strains of Donna Summer's "The Last Dance" meant I had to crawl back home to reality with a weird mixture of exhilaration and despair.)

How I could have used this guidebook to figure out so many of the details of being young, gay, and full of future! Well jump ahead (mutter, mumble, cough) years later and here it is: a self-help book covering the ins and outs of coming out, living, loving, partying, financing, dating, moving in, breaking up, and dating again. And again. And again.

Justin Luke knows the 20something gay experience better than anyone, since he throws NYC's premiere events for just that demographic. He knows how thrilling that period can be because so many experiences are new and exciting in your 20s. Be warned it's also a vulnerable time because your choices will have an impact that will be felt for years to come. And while it's a decade of spontaneity and learning, it's important to not go blindly into the night without the help of people who've been there and made it to the other side. So congrats to Justin for sharing the wisdom—and big kudos to you for wanting to learn how to kiss!

Introduction

Hi there reader.

My name is Justin Luke and I wanted to thank you for buying, stealing, or borrowing this book. Welcome to "The Gay Gospel," a self-help book written specifically for gay 20somethings.

As a recently turned 32-year-old, I have already been through what you are going through now. It isn't easy! Thankfully I made it through those tumultuous years relatively intact. I ended up on the other side with my life on a positive track that is both pleasurable and sustainable. I also have had two years to mull over the ups and downs concerning those tumultuous years.

So dive deep into these pages boys. I'm going to arm you to the teeth with guidance, tips, tools, and some positive truths to help you in both your darkest days and at your highest points.

Please remember that these are only suggestions and recommendations. If something in here rings untrue to you, feel free to disregard it. I am merely giving you advice based on my own personal experiences as well as the lives of gay 20somethings that I observe every night and day at the events that I throw with my company, BoiParty™.

I wish you the best of luck with the years ahead of you boys. I hope that I can offer some small measure of help as you fumble and bumble your way through. So let's begin shall we?

xo JL

The Book of Looking

You Don't NEED A Boyfriend

This is the most important rule when it comes to gay dating. It is a mantra that you absolutely must commit to memory. Chant it while you drive to work or your friend's house party. Remix it with a drumbeat and listen to it while you work out. Write it over and over again in a notebook.

You do NOT need a boyfriend.

If you look at your Facebook newsfeed any hour of the night or day you're likely to come across someone saying "What's wrong with me?" or "Why can't I find the right guy?" or "I need a boyfriend!" or something like that. Bollocks! Incorrect! Feel free to comment on each one and let them know that they're going about it the wrong way.

You need food. You need shelter. You need oxygen. You need clothing. You need money (or a very generous life sponsor). You do NOT need a boyfriend.

Why do you think you need a boyfriend? Is it because you're lonely? Is it because you have a gaping, nerve-filled bloody hole where your dream-significant other is supposed to fit like some sort of fleshy puzzle piece? Will he come into your boyfriend-less world and suddenly make everything magical and perfect?

Don't be silly. A boyfriend is not going to solve your problems. If anything he will add more complexity because you now have someone else besides yourself that you must think about. A boyfriend is not a solution. Never has been, never will be.

Being single should never feel lonely. You have friends. You have family. You have colleagues, and neighbors, and tons of other lovely carbon-based life forms that exist in your life. Furthermore they are happy to have your life enriching theirs. You don't need a boyfriend.

Disclaimer: If you have friends and family and still think you "need" a boyfriend, you will surely become one of those people who ditches their loved ones the second a guy comes along. You've met this kind of person. No one likes this kind of person. They go off into Love Land and come back a few weeks or months later when their shotgun romance takes a bullet in the heart begging for their friends to listen to their problems and help them get over the whole mess. Trust me, no one likes that guy.

When you feel like you need a boyfriend odds are that a boyfriend is actually the LAST thing that you need. What you need is a pet, or a comfy pillow, or a nice long conversation with a loved family member, or a game night with friends where you all drink and have heart-to-hearts with one-another.

What you need to focus on is you. Something is fundamentally wrong with this situation. It means that you aren't a fan of yourself. You get bored when you're alone. There isn't enough excitement or love or intrigue in your life and so you're going to throw that responsibility onto whatever sucker of a guy wanders into your emo tentacles. This will ultimately lead to you suffocating the guy until he runs or lead you to a guy who will suffocate the crap out of you because he's even more co-dependent than you are.

The need for a boyfriend is blinding. It will drive you to date someone that is not right for you. It will cause you to make sacrifices or do dumb things that you need not do just to hang on to this life raft of a guy whom you have convinced yourself is completely and utterly necessary. Ultimately this will lead to a lot of on-again, off-again mini-relationships that will make you even more bitter and jaded. Your "need" for a boyfriend will grow worse and you will find yourself in a destructive, never-ending cycle.

SO STOP THE MADNESS!

Step One: You do not NEED a boyfriend. It's not good enough to think or say it. You need to believe it.

Step Two: Be selfish. Being in a relationship turns "Me" into "We." You will have a harder time improving yourself when you are devoting your attention to your lovely boyfriend/partner. So while you're single, work on you. Improve your career. Improve your body. Read books. Watch films. Take a yoga class.

Step Three: Keep a cool head when a guy appears. The second you realize you don't need a boyfriend the cosmic pinball machine that is the universe will start flinging suitors at you like a demon multi-ball from hell. It always happens. Take a deep breath and remember that you still do not need a boyfriend. This will allow you to go on dates and truly determine if the guy you've met is worth the time and energy that you will invest in him once you start tying the knot.

That's getting ahead a bit. What's important now is the title of this chapter. You do not need a boyfriend. Absolutely no one needs a boyfriend. What you need is to love yourself and enjoy yourself so much that a boyfriend becomes an exciting addition to your already lovely and wonderful life versus a bandage or a tourniquet to stop the dramatic bleeding you imagine you are experiencing.

You do not need a boyfriend. Now go out and tell the world. Every time you repeat it you'll be one step closer to realizing that it's the truth.

You're Not Even LOOKING For a Boyfriend!

I have noticed a recurring phenomenon: boys often are upset because they "can't find a boyfriend." They're "looking for a boyfriend" and all they ultimately find are jerks, crazies, losers, liars, cheats, and porpoises... minus the porpoises. Well I've got some advice for you friends. You need to re-frame!

A wise man once said "Keep your eyes on the prize." Whoever that wise man was... he was an idiot. Keeping your eyes on the prize is like setting a ten year goal. It's too distant. You need to focus more immediately on the present.

I'd like to re-phrase that quote. Let's start saying "Keep your eyes on the process," and "Keep your eyes on the present."

If you do this you might find yourself in less tough, sad, whiny spots. Let me explain. Saying "I'm looking for a boyfriend" is no different than saying "I want to be a millionaire." Well! That's all well and good chap, but how are you gonna do it?

Well if you want to be a millionaire, you might say "I want to be a famous musician!" Okay. And how are you gonna do that? "I want millions of people to download my album!" Okay. And how are you gonna do that? "Well... I need to write an album." Okay. And how will you do that?

"I should probably get started on my first song..." KA-BOOM!

See what I just did there? I broke down "I want to be a millionaire" to its smallest, composite parts. Hell, for some people maybe there's even more composite parts like "I should buy a guitar," or "I should buy a book on songwriting." Let's apply this line of thinking to boyfriends: The boyfriend is the prize. You've got a lot to do before you earn it.

Here is another quick point to remember. A lot of people are fond of saying "I just want a boyfriend... is that so much to ask?" Well let's break it down. I'm guessing that what you mean by boyfriend is:

1. A guy who I find attractive
2. Both inside and out
3. Who ALSO finds me likewise attractive
4. Who keeps me engaged
5. Makes me happy
6. Supports me psychologically
7. Is liked by my friends and family
8. Is honest and loyal
9. Who has some means of living without me so I'm not giving charity
10. Who is good (in my opinion) in bed
11. (add your own additional needs and wants here)

Well that is a helluva lot to ask actually. I'm not saying lower your expectations. I'm saying don't expect him to come falling out of the sky like a dead, sexy bird. The point is simple: you gotta work for that boyfriend. How to guarantee success? Take your eyes off the prize and put them on the process.

What is the process? Well sorry kids, I can't tell you. Everyone is probably going to have separate things that need to be done. Maybe you need to gain some confidence. Maybe you need to get over an ex. Maybe you need to lose some weight or bulk up a bit.

One big thing that is in everyone's boyfriend process is the process of sorting and sifting.

You're separating the wheat from the chaff, sifting through the dirt to find gold. No, I'm not going to say that guys are assholes. I will say that some guys will be assholes to you. Think of us as a bunch of big, gay puzzle pieces. Sometimes two pieces just won't fit together. That doesn't mean that those two pieces can't fit with other pieces.

So think of it as sifting or even shopping. You don't walk into a clothing store and walk out with a pair of jeans without trying them on do you? Likewise you don't buy everything you bring into the changing room with you do you? No you do not. Therefore you're gonna sort and sift. It's like thumping melons at the supermarket. You don't want the ones that are under or over ripe.

My only tip to you as you begin the sorting and sifting is be patient. This will be a lot easier when you realize that you're not looking for a boyfriend. What you're looking for is someone who has the fitting puzzle pieces you find interesting, attractive, and so on. Now once you found him then you can begin seeing if he's a boyfriend candidate. Take your time guys. It's not a race. God ain't making any less gay people.

Go After What You Want

Maybe you're not one of those guys who thinks they need a boyfriend. You would like one. He'd be really swell! You're very well-adjusted and you're prepared to go out and find a suitor. Fabulous! Except there's another issue I've noticed among gay 20somethings: no one wants to make the first move.

Everyone is afraid of being rejected. They think that the guy they want wouldn't be interested in them. So everyone just sorta stands around the club with their friends making lovey-eyes at the guy across the room, sneaking in a smile, and playing coy like they're some 1950's movie starlet at a Sadie Hawkins dance. This is completely inefficient and silly.

Here's the sad thing: the guy you're waiting to come up to you is probably waiting for you to come up to him. You both will go home alone (or with someone else) because neither of you had the balls to make the first move. This is very, very sad.

There is a secret that guys who have the balls to approach people do not want you to know. While you and the cute guy you're eyeing are pretending you're not checking each other out, a guy with a bigger set of cojones will sweep in and nab up either one of you. You've lost your chance and the guy who made the move gets what he wanted.

Yes, there are concerns over rejection. I get that. Let's just start with this simple rule: go after what you want. Be bold. Be brave. You'd be surprised how often it will work out in your favor. If you don't approach the guy you're interested in, you have an almost 100% chance of not getting him. If you do make your move, your chance of success increases very dramatically. So roll the dice, close your eyes, and take the plunge.

The Art of Rejection

If you decide to go out on the prowl, you are going to face rejection. It doesn't matter how cute you feel that night, or how drunk the guy you are talking to might be.

Oh rejection! Fuck you with a capital Fuck You. For something that isn't a physical being you sure as hell inspire a lot of fear and loathing in gays. The fear of not being hot enough, not being interesting enough, being sent back to the part of the bar from where you came... it's so overpowering. It makes you question your attractiveness both inside and out. It has the ability to ruin your night before you've even done anything.

I understand that my recommendation to approach the hot gay guy you just caught sight of is a daunting task. I'm not going to pretend it's easy. It takes a lot of balls. It is difficult. But guess what? It's necessary. Rejection comes in many forms and the moment you get used to it the better you'll be for it.

You need to go out and be rejected. This is the first step to the rest of your life. Next time you're at the bar or the club I challenge you to go up to the smoking hottest guy in the place. The one who wouldn't even look your way if you were on fire and screaming for help.

If he didn't reject you and you're going home together, congrats! Come back to the club next time and try it again. We need to get you rejected outright.

Why? You need to realize rejection is not as bad as we think it is. I believe that our fear of rejection is far worse than the actual feeling of fresh, raw rejection. The best way to get over your fear of it is a bit of exposure therapy: just keep trying to get rejected. Numb the pain. Dull the hit. The more it happens, the less you'll feel it. The day you no longer fear rejection will be the beginning of the rest of your gay life.

Here's the plain truth: very few gays think they're gorgeous (albeit a few choice dickbags on Grindr™). I've met drop-dead gorgeous gays who have astoundingly low self-esteems. Why? I don't know why. No one is fully pleased with themselves. Everyone has parts of them they wish were better. Who succeeds in this world of low-esteemed gay boys? The emboldened ones who are not afraid of rejection succeed.

I'm sorry, but I can't stand idly by while all these pretty boys whine "Where are the good guys? Why can't I find a guy?" To them I say STFU. Because until you surgically remove your fear of rejection and start going after what you want, you deserve to be lonely and depressed. Don't tell me you are single because you come off as "hard to get" or "too hot." You're single because you're a damn coward.

Let me tell you my dream. My dream is a world where gay men are trampling each other in a marathon to get what they want. No pretty boys are waiting to be approached. No boys are scared to approach the man of their dreams due to fear of rejection. I want to create a queer battalion of fearless gay men who go for the boys they're attracted to regardless of how impossible attaining them might seem. Can you do that? Don't let me down!

Allow me to suggest that you should go out with the goal of being rejected. I know I sound crazy. AND MAYBE I AM!!!??? My possible insanity aside, hear me out. If rejection is a regular occurrence when you are searching for a mate, shouldn't you be prepared to face it? Shouldn't you build up a healthy tolerance and bit of gay body armor to defend yourself from rejection's vicious spikes of despair?

So how do you go about getting rejected? It's really easy. Next time you're out and about, go up to whomever you think is the hottest guy there. Walk straight up to him and hit on him. If you get a stinging rejection, good! Savor that feeling. Embrace that cloudy sense that you are a miserable, ugly person who will grow old with no social beings to keep him company except maybe a few dozen Russian nesting dolls that he pretends are real people. Swallow your pride and go hit on the second hottest guy in the room. Lather, rinse, and repeat. I cannot tell you how many times you'll have to be rejected to truly develop a defense to it, but each time you face it you will deal with it better. As I will show you there are many reasons why you will be rejected. Your looks or breath aren't the only excuse. Minimize the "Rejection Monster" and you'll be that much better off.

I know what you are thinking. What if the hottest or second hottest guy in the room doesn't reject you? Well congratulations. Enjoy it and go out and try to get rejected again the next night. It will come.

Ten Reasons You'll Be Rejected

Okay it's still tough approaching a guy somewhere. So let's get the monster out in the open so we can learn how best to kill it. Let's look at some of the many reasons why you may be rejected. The point of this exercise is to defuse the fear. When we fear rejection, we are really afraid of being made to feel unattractive/hideous/wildebeest-like. We're not afraid of the act of being turned down. We are afraid of the feelings of self-loathing it conjures inside of us.

Guess what friends? Your not being cute enough is only one of the many reasons you may be rejected. Until scientists develop a technology that allows us to see into someone's life and head, we're just going to have to take a chance.

So here we go. You may get rejected by that hot guy because of any one of the following:

1. He has a boyfriend.
Not every gay guy is single! Something I was guilty of doing in my single days was assuming that every hot guy I saw was unattached and ready for loving. Clearly that is untrue. Unless the guy is in an open relationship, a lying cheat, or dating a girl and diddling on the side, chances are he will reject your advances.

2. He's on the verge of having a boyfriend.

Maybe that guy's been exchanging texts and emails with a guy he met a few weeks ago. He thinks he's got this in the bag. He may be single now, but he doesn't think it will be this way for much longer. He probably couldn't care less about you because he's so very close to marital bliss.

3. He just broke up with a boyfriend.

While people like to talk about rebounds and jumping in bed with someone after a bad breakup that's not always the case. Sometimes the heartbroken gay wants nothing to do with gay men ever again (for a few weeks at least). He's certainly not about to let you anywhere near his shattered heart. Chances are that he's also a little emotionally and mentally unstable presently…. he's doing you a favor by not getting you wrapped up in all of that.

4. He's visiting town.

Tourists are a big thing in any major metropolitan area. The guy you're scoping out might be from out of town, state, or country. Now while a one-night stand may be in the cards, he may not be into that. If he's not into that, then he's not going to be into you. He's probably too busy trying to remember all the things he will have to pack before he heads home.

5. He has an STD.

Eek! Syphilis! Gonorrhea! Crabs! Nothing you want right? Well they're here. Imagine HAVING them and knowing about it. Maybe he recently got diagnosed. Maybe it burned when he peed this morning. A guy might turn you down because he doesn't want to give you anything. This is a very sweet gesture that you should appreciate.

6. He's got life drama.

What if the guy just had a death in his family? A horrible fight with a best friend? Lost a job? Lost his house? Got robbed or mugged? Maybe his favorite television character died the other night. Any potential terrible event may be plaguing their mind thoroughly occupying it and thus squeezing you out.

7. He doesn't think you're cute.

Okay, it had to be said. Maybe you're not the guy's type. Whoops! Hit to the ego. FUCK that hurts. He's being a bitch about it too, rolling his eyes like you should know you don't stand a chance with him. Take your lumps, swallow hard, and head off to approach your next guy.

8. He's heard shit about you.

Do you have a bad rep? Do you have someone who hates you enough to manufacture a bad rep? You never know what might have been said about you to this guy or that. Maybe he heard that you shoot loads in people's eyes and then flee the scene. Maybe he heard you have a horrible rash. Whatever. Perhaps you should guard your reputation more carefully. Another viable option is to take the time to mend your reputation and show him you're not whatever he's heard.

9. He's just not looking.

Believe it or not some guys are just not looking for a date or hook up. For whatever reason, right now they're just there to dance, or drink, or catch up with friends. They're not looking and so you best look elsewhere.

10. He's not ready for you yet.

This is key boys. Sometimes a hook-up/date is just not in the cards for tonight. Take a deep breath, accept your rejection like a man, and soldier on. There are many more nights, many more weeks, many more months, many more years. Guys that once rejected me were the same guys that went home with me months later. (I actually once went home with a guy who rejected me a decade previous). "No" today doesn't mean "No" forever.

There you have it. Ten fresh reasons why you may get rejected by that guy that's got you drooling and dreaming of monogrammed bathrobes and a tastefully sized dog. Only one of those reasons having to do with you not being cute enough.

In other words, there are a ton of reasons why you will be rejected by that guy. But so what? There's also the chance that you will get him because you're his type... or you're his type tonight. You'll never know if you don't gather your balls and approach. So stop standing there and staring, stop feeling down on yourself, and stop being a pussy. Get out there and go for it!

Someone For Everyone

Wow. Those past two chapters were an awful lot of rejection weren't they? Even I'm feeling a little bit down and unlovable and perhaps doomed to spend the rest of my life alone. Relax! There is hope.

I'm sure you've been through a large pile of Rat Bastards, Dirty Cheaters, Flakey McFlakersons, and every sort of jackass in between. That's part of the game though. Rest assured there is someone out there for you. The better news? There isn't only one of him! There's a whole bunch of guys out there who are perfectly complimentary to you and will be your ideal mate for many years to come.

The thing is that you have to go out and find him. Let's say there are about one hundred or so guys who are perfect for you. That's not that many when compared to the millions of gay men around the world. This means that there is a lot of sifting and digging you're going to have to do.

You're only doomed to be alone if you give up on your quest for that special someone who uniquely fits with you. It's just like any job, task, or challenge: get up after you fall off the horse and go for your next ride. There's no guarantee when you'll find the right guy, but you will. You always will. And every time you fall, you'll have learned a little more about the game. You'll have a clearer idea of the kind of guy you want and the kind of guy you are. By the time you meet this perfect guy it may be that if you had met him at the beginning of your journey, he never would have qualified as the one you would want to spend the rest of your life with. And likewise you may not have been his first choice either. But you both will have come a long way and learned a lot about yourselves and what you actually want from a partner. And so a partnership would come from experience, a journey, some life-lessons, and just a drop of luck that you met each other when you did.

There is someone out there for you. If you're in your twenties, relax. I didn't meet my current life partner Joe until I turned twenty-eight years old. I came out of the closet and started dating guys when I was seventeen years old. That's eleven years of searching high and low to find the right guy, and finding every single matter of wrong guy along the way.

No matter what you look like or what parts of you are great (or not so great) there is someone out there who's looking for someone just like you. Even if you're slightly off from what he pictures to be the perfect guy he will be uniquely equipped to work with you to meet you in the middle because chances are he won't be the perfect replica of what you've imagined either.

Don't believe me? That's fine. You'll find out as the years pass and one day you meet him. By that time you may have forgotten that I told you this guy was out there. That's okay. I'll still have been right and that's all that matters.

Be Bold; Be You

The problem with most gay men dating in their twenties is that they are often absolutely convinced that this guy they landed will be their last chance at happiness forever. He is pure perfection, and he's the last lifeboat coming along before a flood of solitude and loneliness rises above their head and drowns them forever. How emo and completely ridiculous. There will always be another guy. There will always be another date. There will always be another chance.

The worst thing that comes of this perceived desperation is that guys are willing to sacrifice any part of them in order to not alienate the guy they're seeing. They will hide parts of them that they think aren't palatable. They will not hold their own in arguments or will be willing to do anything just to prevent any problems.

Don't do that.

If the person you are portraying is not actually you, you need to cut that crap out immediately. You may think that it's helping to seal the deal on the guy so you can hurry up and get married and not be alone for the rest of your life, but you are woefully wrong.

What you are actually doing is giving a dishonest perspective on who you are, thus throwing off the natural course of your relationship. If you are not compatible with the guy you have started seeing, it's best that you figure this out immediately or at least as soon as possible so that you both can cut your losses and go back out into the dating world.

Furthermore pretending to be something you aren't is a short-sighted strategy. As your relationship continues to get serious, the real you will ultimately come out. There may be certain things that you need from a mate that you pretended you did not need and one day you will need it so bad that the truth will come out. If this ends up being a large enough mountain between you and your guy, your relationship will go down the tubes.

If you spend a long time not being yourself and ultimately end up losing the relationship, you'll never know how many compatible guys you could have had a genuine connection with have come and gone. The guy who was completely and truly perfect for you may have met someone else while you were wasting time trying to fit a square peg in a round hole.

I'm not saying you should come out swinging at the guy you're seeing and being very forceful about who you are and what you want. There's always an art of compromise in a relationship, but "yourself" is not a compromise that you are allowed to make.

This also goes for physical qualities. I personally have always struggled with my weight. I hate gyms with a passion and I love food. I diet and try to eat right and have kept myself in a healthy weight range for quite some time (with the occasional lapse... damn you pizza!) But the point is I know I'll never be some sexy trim or super buff beast and I'm okay with that. I found a guy who wasn't looking for a muscle monster, and we're very happy together. So whatever you are someone will be into that. It may take a while, but so does anything that's worth it.

Be you and be proud about it. As long as you're happy with what and who you are, you will find someone else who is too.

Hardcore Text

You gave a guy your number. You flirted and maybe made out and maybe slept together. From there you took it to the world of text messaging. Cute lil mwah mwah kissy-kissy's sent back and forth to each other with the help of satellites in space. So adorable!

Then... something goes wrong. The dude of your dreams stops responding. For hours and days at a time. What happened!? You texted each other every morning and afternoon and evening.

Where did he go? I don't know. What I can tell you is how long is too long for him to not respond to you: Twelve hours. Short! Crazy! Ridiculous... right? Wrong. Completely wrong. This is a very fair amount of time to give your Text Buddy. If a guy does not text you back within that allotted time, he is either over you, into someone else, or dead.

When I hear tales of guys going radio silent for a few days and then returning saying "I'm sorry. I was busy," I yank out a little bit of my hair. Luckily my hair is full and oft-growing so no bald spot has appeared. Why do I become so frustrated? Because everywhere I go I see one thing: people texting. We're at dinner with friends... and texting. We're dancing at the club... and texting. We're walking through the streets and falling down subway entrances because we are texting.

Face the truth boys. Everyone texts all the goddamn time. If he isn't texting you, he is guaranteed "Not That Into You." It takes five seconds to send a smiley and say you're busy. Considering how much time people spend taking photos of themselves on Facebook or complaining that they're bored... this is but a tiny time investment.

Wait! Maybe there is a good reason for his silence. Perhaps. But never more than twelve hours since your last text. The following reasons are excuse for an absence of texting with variable times that seem pretty accurate:

He's seeing a movie or show.

Acceptable duration: Up to three hours.

This is actually very generous because what movie is three hours nowadays?

His phone died.

Acceptable duration: Up to eight hours.

Because like any person with a cell phone, he'll run to a charger as soon as he can and immediately reach out to anyone he missed communications from.

He lost his phone.

Acceptable duration: Up to twenty-four hours.

Before twenty-four hours passes he will make that Facebook event invite asking you for your number. You don't have his Facebook? Well that was stupid.

He's on a cruise or traveling across Europe.

Acceptable duration: One-two weeks.

If he didn't bother to tell you this ahead of time, he STILL isn't all that into you.

He's been kidnapped and/or killed.

Acceptable duration: Forever

Sad, I know. Also extremely rare!

And that's it! I'll say it again Mission Impossible style. This Text Message Relationship will self-destruct in twelve hours. Better get those fingers flapping. If he doesn't text you back within twelve hours, you have permission to send a clarification text to make sure he got the original. If he still doesn't respond, just delete his number. It's over, whatever it was.

Ten Reasons NOT to Go Home with That Guy

You're drunk, he's drunk. You're horny, he's horny. It's getting late. You're getting hornier. You take his hand and whisper into his ear: "Wanna get outta here?"

He nods. You smile, and lead him to the door…

HOOOOOOLD UP buddy! Bringing a sexy stranger home with you (or going home with them) is risky business, and not in the STD-way (well, not only in that way). Have you fully considered some of the possible outcomes?

Here are some things to consider:

1. He's not as cute as you think.

Be sure to get your boy of the night in some bright light. Even halogen, ugly lights like the kinds in all-night diners and electronics stores. The ones that could make anyone look hideous. Club lighting is very generous with all of its colors and angles and flashiness. It could make a barstool look gorgeous. So double-check with a friend or two. You want to be absolutely sure you're taking home what you are actually seeing and not what you think you see.

2. He may be a clinger.

Stage 1! Stage 1! You wake up in the A.M. and he's cuddling you like you've been married for a decade and your kids are screaming in the next room. He wants breakfast. He has made lunch plans. He crocheted you a pair of socks in the shape of your sleeping face while you were unconscious. Choosing a clinger is always a risk and not something you can tell up front.

3. You may not be sexually compatible.

It's totally okay to ask the guy if he's a top or bottom before you ask him home. And no, it's not rude or brash. You're about to ask him if he'll come home with you so you can get naked and suck and fuck each other. To ask where he likes to put what is hardly an inappropriate question. Don't think you can divine this information. Just because he's bouncing his booty on you does not mean he's a bottom. Check first.

4. He might not look as good naked.

I know that some people are looking for pure physical perfection where one night stands are concerned. I support this. You're not looking for a husband, you're looking for nookie. So shouldn't this be the shallowest of decisions? Give him a squeeze here, there, and over there. Make sure he's not hiding things you don't like or find a turn off under a scientifically augmented pair of undies or shirt.

5. You have something important to do tomorrow.

Is something big happening on the horizon? A meeting? A job interview? An audition? Be responsible. If you can get him tonight, you can get him another night. Be smart and acknowledge that there are some things that are more important than sex.

6. He may be too drunk.

Whiskey dick? No, no, no. First of all, it's creepy and slightly evil to get it on with a guy who's smashed. You don't want to wake up in the morning to find him screaming next to you in bed. Also, if he can't get it up, keep his eyes open, or move his body without vomiting, chances are you don't want him in bed with you.

7. He may have a boyfriend.

Cheaters! Liars! Guess what? They exist. I suggest you ask him and maybe some other people point blank. You don't want to get your balls entwined in the brambles of drama by poking someone else's man. He may even claim to have an open relationship, but that might not be true.

8. They could be a package deal you never wanted.

See that hot guy? He may have a spooky silent secret partner that comes along with the deal. It's a sort of unwanted bonus you don't discover until you get to his place and a dead ringer for Daddy Warbucks or a straight, female girlfriend or a boyfriend you don't find half as cute is waiting there, winking at you.

9. You don't know where they live.

Going home with someone is a commitment, and one that's not easily broken. What if his home is in shambles? Or he's roommates with a crazy person? Or he lives somewhere not near a subway? Be very careful to know where you're going before you go there.

10. He may be a thief.

Imagine waking up to find out that your one night stand stole shit from your apartment including one of your nightstands! Don't think this is impossible. I know people it's happened to. It's always good to do an impromptu background check. See if he knows anyone you know, and that the person you know can vouch for him.

Just be sure to think through these things before you commit to going home with that guy. Be safe, be smart, and be sure you know someone who knows them. It can help you eliminate many of these problems.

We're ALL Fucked Up

Perhaps you feel like you're broken beyond repair. You lost a family member or you had a relationship that self-destructed. Your ears are too flappy or you have anxiety or depression or OCD or ADHD. Whatever it is, it is clearly a big deal and you are irreparably damaged for the rest of eternity.

Guess what? So is absolutely everyone else.

No one thinks they're amazing and perfect, even if they're forever posting underwear selfies on Facebook, and even if they strut down the street like they own the place. Everyone including you, me, and everyone has moments, minutes, hours, days where they can barely even look at themselves in the mirror without wanting to break down into tears.

Why? I don't know. But this is the simple truth: we are all fucked up. For whatever reason, due to whatever circumstances. No one gets a free pass out of this sort of occasional self-loathing. Hot guys may feel stupid. Rich guys may feel ugly. Powerful guys may feel lonely.

We are all damaged beings. So don't let that stop you from going after what you want. Just remember this: finding someone else will not help you fix you. Only you can fix you. And just because you're occasionally down doesn't indicate an irreparable issue. We all get like that. It's part of being alive.

The Ultimate Pick-Up Line

You're on the prowl. You've decided it's time to find yourself a mate whether it's for forever or for the night until the tequila wears off. Now what? You're at the club, or the bar, or at a house party and you've seen Mr. Right (or Prince Right Now, or Captain Right Now, and Maybe Later Too). You lock eyes, or your eyes lock on his chest. What do you do?

You've heard tons of pick-up lines over your life. Most of them are hilarious, corny, or overused. You might think that an old fashioned "Hi!" or "Hey, how are you?" would be fine, and it very well may be. Unfortunately you then run the chance that you will end up in an intense conversation and have to forcibly steer it towards a pick-up line of some kind. It can be a pain to hijack a conversation to let your conversational partner know that your interest in him goes a little deeper than his opinions on what's happening in Syria or on men's fashion.

I've got a secret for you. It is the Ultimate Pick-Up Line. I have perfected it over years of experimenting. I have compared it to other supposed Ultimate Pick-Up lines, and it has stood champion with other failed contenders convulsing and coughing up blood at its feet.

Notice I didn't call it a magical line. It isn't some incantation (Hotsus Datesus!) that will make the man you use it on fall for you on the spot. I will not guarantee you success at a higher percentage than with any other pick-up line. In fact, it might end up getting you rejected (which, as we've discussed, is still good).

The Ultimate Pick-Up Line

But I will guarantee you a lot of saved time and fumbling. This is the Ultimate Pick-Up Line because it is extraordinarily efficient.

Are you ready?

Just walk up to the guy you're interested in and say the following words:

"Hey, you're really cute."

It works even better if you couple it with a sexy and suggestive, sorta-cute grin or smirk.

Bold? Brave? Forward? Yes, yes, and hells yes.

It's more effective than you could ever guess. When you drop this line you have done a whole host of things at once. For one, you've cut through the clutter and stated your intentions. You are physically attracted to the person. You are brave enough to approach them and put your neck on the chopping block, and you have handed them the axe.

Most of the guys I meet out in the world are socially submissive. Even the hottest guy in the room, believe it or not, is most likely petrified to make the first approach. It blows my mind that this is the case, but there you have it. The small group of gays who are bold enough to go in and make the first approach have an alarming success rate. The Early Bird gets the worm and all of that.

So gather up your balls and go tell the guy "Hey, you're really cute."

This will get you one of two basic responses:

1. "Hahahahaha! (blushes) You're pretty cute yourself." (sexy eyes)
2. "Thanks so much!" (walks away)

Number two is assuming that the guy you've approached isn't a jerk. Occasionally, number two could turn out to be a real big number two complete with bitch face, eye rolls, huffs, and stomping off. It'll hurt, but you'll live to say the line another day.

The point of this Ultimate Pick-Up Line is that it cuts all the crap and gets to the point. You give the guy a "Yes or No" question, and you will get a "Yes or No" response. There's no need to wonder what he thinks about you or if the full-blown conversation you are engaging in can take a turn for the sexual or romantic.

Try the line out a few times not in the mirror, but when you're out. Pick a cute guy and take a chance. Then keep on trying. I'm not promising you that it will work, but I can promise you that you'll save yourself a lot of wasted time.

Going Home with a Straight Guy

This chapter wasn't originally in this book. In my ten-plus years of gay dating and hooking up I have never gone home with someone who identified as straight. The closest I came was getting it on with guys of the hetero variety when I was in high school experimenting with guy friends who are now all married. But I have heard an outcry from many of my friends recently: you need to talk about going home with a straight guy!

First, let me say that I am not one to render judgment. I do believe that sexuality is a very fluid thing. A man can be straight and do something with a guy once or twice in his life as an experiment without being branded as a homosexual. Just like drunken college girls can make out with each other at the fraternity beer beach blast without being known as lesbians for the rest of their lives. So let's go ahead and shake the judgment and the desire to slap a label on everything and just go with the flow.

From speaking to many different guys on the scene I have ascertained that there are four types of straight guys that you may encounter either online or out in public who will go home with you, or bring you home with them. Here they are:

1. The First-Timer

This is the freshest form of hetero dude that you may encounter. Maybe he's had thoughts or ideas or maybe he's just so drunk and something in his head clicked. Maybe he did something a long time ago or maybe the idea never hit him until that very night. There's no way of knowing. There are a few things you can expect. For one, don't expect any sort of homosexual talent. There will be teeth. There may be nails. There may be blood. There will likely not be the sort of cleanliness you might come to expect from someone you go home with. He may chicken out or freak out before it even happens. You are dealing with a very vulnerable and volatile person. I recommend you stay away from this type of guy unless you're in a teaching mood.

2. The Clinger Caterpillar

Maybe he's done this before, maybe he hasn't. But once you are done with him, he becomes completely attached to you. He's not gay. He's just straight with "You tendencies." Be careful of this one because he may lure you into a sense of false romance that will not ever come to be. He also may be emotionally unstable considering he is teetering on his very understanding of his gender preferences. You will be his only solace, and you will be a full-time volunteer psychotherapist. If you notice clinginess after your first rendezvous, it may be wise to call it a one-nighter and high-tail it out of there.

3. The Chatty Cathy

This guy is going to get deep inside of you... but only through your ears. He seemed ready for Right Now at the bar or club, but you get him back home and discover that all he really wanted to do was talk. He wants to tell you about how torn he is about his sexuality. Maybe he will recount to you every sexual experiment he's undergone since he started playing around. This will go on for quite a few hours. Before you know it the sun will be up and your eyelids will be filled with sandbags. No sex and a ton of pillow talk. If this is something you're interested in, go ahead and enjoy. But if you have a certain idea of how the night should go, perhaps you should go somewhere else.

4. The Pretender

Some of the "straight" guys you go home with will actually, clearly, beyond evidently be gay. Why won't they admit it? Maybe they don't know it or maybe they know it but can't come to terms with it. Whatever the reason that's none of your business. You wanted to go home with a "straight" boy and so here you are. Sex with him should be fantastic because this clearly isn't his first time at the Top'N'Bottom Rodeo, but do not get attached. Please don't. It will not end well. He won't be turning gay for you. And if he does, you have a lot of steps and complications ahead of you. Why not pick a model that's plug-n-play ready?

The Spinning Wheels of Gay Dating

I feel bad telling you to go and get rejected without giving you a bit more support in your emotionally suicidal mission. So allow me to arm you with some more advice. Over the years I have met many, many guys who are chasing after somebody. And by many guys, I mean most guys. It's as rare as a winning lotto ticket to find someone who is single and not looking.

It sort of works out like this:

Guy X: "Oh God, Justin. I am so into Guy Y. He's so gorgeous. And we've been kinda flirting, sorta, or something. I think he likes me! But he's not answering my texts. I just don't know."

Ten minutes later… here comes Guy Y with a concerned expression on his face.

Guy Y: "Justin! I need your help getting Guy Z's attention. I don't understand why he won't give me the time of day. We're perfect for each other! Can you fix it?"

Ten minutes later… here comes Guy Z with an apathetic look adorning his face.

Guy Z: "Hey Justin! Can I get a drink ticket? I just fucked my ex and I need to get wasted so I don't go back to his place and do it again."

And now you too can see the tragedy unfold. Guy Y is preoccupied with Guy Z and doesn't even know (nor necessarily care) that Guy X is hot for him and would do anything to have him. To make matters more complex there's a very good chance that Guy Z is chasing after someone and someone else is likewise chasing after Guy X.

In television and film we get a lot of love triangles. This guy likes that girl but so does that other guy! Oh no! What will they do!? A love triangle would be a lot better to be honest. In the gay community we have infinite, separate spinning circles. There are no connecting points anywhere. This guy likes that guy, who likes that other guy, who likes that other-other guy, and on and on into infinity and beyond.

This is the reality of gay dating. We are all chasing one-another and very rarely are we chasing the guy who is chasing us. So we are all hamsters on exercise wheels, forever running forward but never getting anywhere.

Why do we do this? I haven't figured that part out yet either. Sure some psychologist could bungee-jump in through the ceiling and say that "We only want what we can't have," but I think that's overgeneralizing. In all honesty I think it's a sort of wrong-place, wrong-time situation. Our attention is drawn somewhere to some dream guy, and suddenly we are blind to those around us. Even if a perfectly wonderful suitor arrives, we are already obsessed or otherwise occupied with the original guy we were chasing. It's a sad truth, but it's a truth nonetheless.

I wish I could give you a solution to this problem, but there really isn't one. As a community we will always chase and be chased, and only rarely will we collide head-on with someone who is also chasing us. The best thing you can do is keep your spirits high, continue improving yourself whenever you can, and resting assured that someday you will bang head-first into the guy who you were chasing because he was sprinting at you just as quickly.

If you really want a different answer, allow me to dare say that you should take a step back, quiet yourself for a second, and try to figure out if someone is chasing you. I'm telling you right now that someone probably is. You're just not realizing it. He's texting or Facebook messaging you and you send him a response sometimes while you're pining for Guy Y or Z or whoever.

Once you ascertain that someone is in pursuit of you stop spinning and think about it. Would you rather keep chasing whomever it is you're running after in hopes that he'll stop chasing his target and turn around and notice you? Or would you prefer to cut your losses and give the guy chasing you a chance?

Game Over

"I'm sick of guys playing games!" I swear to God I see this status update pop up on my Facebook timeline every day if not every hour. More often than not the people posting this are guilty of playing games with guys as well.

Can we all just agree to stop playing games? Perhaps it'll help to identify what "playing games" even means. In my opinion, playing games boils down to behaving either deceitfully or un-naturally. It's waiting to text or call someone when you would call them more quickly in any other social situation. It's choosing to refrain from telling someone that you aren't interested in them, for whatever terrible (or well-intended) reason thereby causing confusion. It's not telling someone you are interested in them and instead keeping your true goals, dreams, and motives secret.

In other words, "Playing Games" is actually a really nice, fun way of saying "being a deceitful, lying coward." Strong words? Yes. But that's what it is, boys.

How do you stop playing games? Just be honest! Be upfront. Be yourself. If you like a guy, tell him you like him. If a guy tells you that he likes you but you don't like him, tell him. Don't wait for him to text or call you if you want to speak with him… just text or call him. If someone texts or calls you, don't play hard to get and delay your response. Call or text him back!

Our lives are busy and harried enough. Having a crush on a guy is a lovely distraction from other issues that we have every single day. When games enter the courtship and possible-dating world, suddenly these interactions become just as stressful as our daily travails.

The other problem with games is that everyone has a different understanding of what the rules are! What's the correct amount of days for me to wait to call him after we had that awesome movie date? How many times do I let him say he loves me before I tell him I'm actually making out with his twin brother? This is too complicated, too stressful, and a patent waste of time.

Stop with the games. And if you're currently interacting with someone who is playing games with you, call him out, see if he mends his ways. If he doesn't, ditch him and go find someone else. You'll thank me in the long run.

If we all could agree to place a moratorium on game-playing, our lives would become that much better. So why not start the trend? Be honest. Be yourself. Respect each other. Make our dating world a better place.

To Catch a Catfish

I'm not entirely old-fashioned. Once upon a time, meeting someone online was a huge stigma that many had to face. People believed that relationships forged from online personals were somehow inauthentic, phony, or downright wrong. Well, time is the Grand Decider and online-first relationships have almost completely shaken their negative connotations. With the emergence of mobile hook-up apps and online dating sites, it seems that more and more people are using the interwebz as a digital cupid. I'm totally cool with this. Not all of us are equipped or able to go out into the world and find someone. And if we can order groceries, dinner, movies, books, and anything else we want to be delivered directly to our residence, why should potential husbands be any different?

One thing still remains from the early, dark days of online dating: The Wily Catfish. A catfish, in case you don't have MTV or never saw the original documentary, is a person who uses someone else's photos and claims that he is someone else to deceive whomever he is talking to. It may be hard to believe that the person you're talking to is not who they claim they are, but that's a very distinct possibility. Here are some ways to make sure that the guy you're chatting with is the real deal.

Their profile photo isn't a person.

The easiest giveaway is if the person has not ever used their actual face for a profile photo. Then again, who's going to fall in love with a drawing of Betty Boop? That's an easy ringer. Plus they're not necessarily a catfish because they're not claiming to be a cartoon character, or an AIDS ribbon, or an equality sign, or whatever they've chosen.

They don't have enough profile photos.

There are a ton of gorgeous guys all over Facebook. Thing is a lot of them only have one or two profile photos. These are fake people. Most people don't fall for this any longer, but some still do. Take a click through of their profile photos. If there is only a small handful of them, you're probably talking to a catfish.

Their profile photos are very old.

I don't think it's asking much that someone change their profile photo every few months. Most people do. If the guy you're talking to has a few profile photos but they are all dated from 2012 or earlier, that's either not him or he hasn't aged so well. Either way it's deceitful, so be careful.

The lonely wall.

Is the guy you're talking to only ever posting status updates on his own? Tread carefully. Any normal human on Facebook is going out and about. He's being tagged by friends at clubs, or parties, or restaurants, or movies. He's probably been tagged in some family or friend photos, as well. If the guy you're talking to is just posting his own stuff and is never tagged by anyone anywhere, you've got yourself a catfish.

The Eight-Hour test.

Want to figure out if you're dealing with a catfish right now to save yourself wasted time or a horrible murder later down the road? Send him a message and request that he immediately send you a photo of himself holding a piece of paper with a message written on it. Pick whatever message you want. Now, he might be at work or something, so you can grant him the leeway to snap this photo. In this day and age we are always near a camera, paper, and a pen. He can use his phone, iPod, tablet, or computer. It's not that difficult. Also any normal, real person would simply say "Sure!" and send you the photo. It takes but a few seconds. If the guy fights with you about it or tries to come up with excuses, it's a catfish. Drop him. Block him. Move on.

At best, a catfish is an annoying waste of your time and emotions. At worst, he could be a psychopathic killer or a dangerous individual. Keep an eye out and be wary.

The Book of Dating

The First Date

You've been rejected, you've come back to the well over and over again, and finally, just when it seemed like it would never happen–it happens! That cute guy you met at your friend's Ugly Christmas Sweater house party gave you his phone number and asked you to hit him up. Well, now what?

Planning the date.

I'll give you some golden advice. Don't add him on Facebook. Don't follow him on Twitter. Don't shoot him a text message or search for his defunct LinkedIn page. Call him the next day. Call him and ask him out. Old fashioned? You bet! It's also still the best way to go about this.

Disclaimer: If you've met this guy online (Facebook, Grindr, wherever, I don't judge) your mission is to get them out of the digital space and into the real world as soon as possible. The longer you exist in the zeros and ones of the Internet, the less likely it will be that you two will ever have a chance to date. You'll just chat back and forth, never commit, and then one night you'll see him out at a club, or bar, or the movies with another guy. You missed your shot and it will suck a lot. So don't blow it.

Get the boy on the phone like it's an old sitcom and you had to ask the operator to connect you to Ms. McGillicutty across the way. Connect your voices and ask him out.

Where? Dinner or coffee. No movies. No gay bars. No gay clubs.

As a nightlife promoter and a lover of films I am not saying that there is anything wrong with any of the three aforementioned activities, but they are not at all suitable for a first date. You don't want a chance for your or their eyes to wander to a cute guy passing by or for a friend to appear out of the blue and suddenly you've got a third wheel. Likewise, you don't want to spend a few hours together noshing on popcorn and not staring into one-another's eyes. That's for later in your dating journey.

For the first date you want a restaurant or a coffee place (or a wine bar, that works too). You want to sit and have minimal distractions. Save the scenic walks and bowling and entertainment places for later dates as well. The first date is a very serious one, and you need your full attention spent on each other.

Before the date.

No peeking on Facebook or other social media sites! No asking your friends who knows what about him. That's like opening Christmas presents before Christmas morning. It's like reading the end of a book before you've seen the first page. Leave some mystery and excitement. Give yourself things that you'll want to find out. The more you go into the date knowing, the less you'll have to talk about and to discover about each other.

The date.

A first date is like a first job interview. Think of yourself as a Human Resources specialist. Your first exposure to the candidate was the resume/cover letter and now you're going to feel him out to see if he's a good fit for the company that is your heart. Put your phone away. Try your best not to check out other guys that walk by. And most importantly, ask lots of questions.

I said this was like a job interview. Well don't you want to get a good feeling for the candidate? Ask him about his life, his job, his family. Where did he come from? What would he rather be doing? You want to talk as little about yourself as possible. This is all about getting to know him.

I hope for your sake that your date asks you as many questions as you are asking him. If you're just lobbing questions at him and getting monosyllable responses back, you're probably better off going home and talking to Siri (at least she can tell you some pretty interesting stuff about foreign planets and things).

Sex?

This part is all up to you boys. I know successful relationships that went balls-deep in each other on the first night, and I know couples that waited weeks before they even saw each other with their shirts off.

It is an unavoidable fact that sexual chemistry is a very important part of a relationship. Are you big enough? Is he? Do each of you want the same thing? Are you attentive or rough or cute or wild enough? This will ultimately be decided on the field by which I mean the bed (or floor, or counter, or...)

Disclaimer: Yes, couples do learn each other's ticks and tocks as time goes on. Don't just write your guy off if he didn't hit each and every one of your magic spots. Give him a shot or two. Especially if the rest of the date went so well.

Second date?

This is going to be up to the both of you (duh). But before you ask him on a second date or agree to go back out with him, run through the date in your head. Did you like what you learned about him? Did you truly enjoy yourself? Did he make you feel important? Did you want to make him feel important? If you feel good about it, go forth and schedule that second date.

Keep It Positive

Trust me on this point: the last thing you want to bring with you on a date is the metaphoric tiny violin. I don't care how many guys have done you wrong and neither does the guy you're sitting across the table from. When you start dating someone, keep things positive. I'm not saying to lie. If you've had a bad day, I invite you to share that with the guy you're talking to, but be very careful that you don't descend quickly into "Womp Womp" territory.

There's nothing that kills a date quicker than someone being a Negative Nancy. My mom taught me a very good lesson: if you don't have something nice to say, don't say anything at all. Allow me to adapt it and switch out the word "nice" for the more important word "positive."

You want to show your new guy all of your good qualities. You're funny! You're insightful! You're intelligent! You're creative! You can yodel! These are good things you can leave behind as memories for the guy when the night comes to an end. You do not want him walking away remembering the negatives. You're whiny! You're still heartbroken from the last guy you saw! You have a terrible job that you hate and want to get out of! You might be bipolar! If any of these things are true about you, that's totally fine as well. Just don't let them slip yet. Your guy can discover these further down the line. Probably around the point when you can keep the bathroom door open while you're talking because he's in the living room and you don't want to cut off your conversation.

If you find that you're having a hard time staying positive on this date, then perhaps you need to reconsider what the hell you're doing. If you were a pitcher with a fractured shoulder, the captain wouldn't send you to the mound. If you're still emo and negative about a previous relationship, then you aren't playing your A-Game and perhaps you need a little bit longer in the "Single Oven" before you come back out as a date-ready bundt cake.

Here's another trick: even if you've had a crappy day, or week, or life, take comfort in the fact that you're currently out with someone who would like to get to know you better and maybe spend more time with you in the future. Isn't that nice!? It's a very hopeful thing to remember. Cling to that. Not all is wrong in the world. But if you continue with your whiny, tiny violin, you better be ready for this guy to hit the road and find someone with a happier outlook on life.

Let's look at this from the other side. If you're out on a date and your guy seems to be down in the dumps, I would err on the side of giving him the benefit of the doubt. Try and cheer him up. Be there for him. Do so for this first date at least. If by your second date you find that he's still a grumpy, depressed Womp Womp of a guy, I suggest you run for the hills. You will save yourself a lot of pain and torment and mood swings in the future. And, who knows, maybe his losing a guy as nice as you might clue him in that he needs to work on his outlook on life before he ventures back out into the dating world.

Find His Flaws... Fast

Every single human being on this planet has flaws. There are so many millions of different flaws out there that I'm pretty sure not all of them have been catalogued just yet. You have flaws. The guy you're currently courting also has flaws. I have flaws. My boyfriend has flaws. My friends and coworkers and everyone on this planet does.

So go out and find some flaws. If you find yourself saying, posting, or thinking "I've met the most absolutely perfect guy in the world! He's the one! He's flawless!" then you are very wrong and you clearly haven't spent much time with one-another. Fix that fast.

I'm not pointing this out to put a damper on your happiness. In fact I am doing quite the opposite. While everyone has flaws the good thing is that there are people out there whose flaws you won't give a damn about. The most perfect couples are ones whose flaws don't matter to each other and whose amazing qualities are exactly what each of them is looking for.

My point is simple: your guy has flaws and probably quite a few of them. You need to go rooting and searching to find out what his exact flaws are so you can make sure that they aren't deal-breakers for you. Likewise, he's looking into you trying to determine your flaws as well just to make sure that he can stand you at your unique form of worst.

Let me say this again: flaws are not horrible by design or default. The fact that he bites his fingernails might have driven his ex insane, but you might not really care or you might bite your nails too. Maybe he snores, but you're a super-deep sleeper. In fact what may be a flaw to one man may not be a flaw to another; like that whole "one man's trash is another man's treasure" thing. Maybe you watch a ton of reality TV and hate reading. To someone that might be the worst flaw in the world. To someone else that guarantees you two will spend a happy eternity together skipping book clubs so you can see the latest psychopaths on reality TV.

How do you hunt for flaws? Easy! Spend time with the guy and pay attention while you do so. The more situations and scenarios you find yourselves in, the more opportunities will come about for the flaws to surface and present themselves. Then you can make decisions as the parade of flaws begins. Namely are these deal-breakers or are they no big deal whatsoever?

You and your guy will ultimately be the judge.

(Not) Going the Distance

It is said that absence makes the heart grow fonder. I agree! Whenever my boyfriend goes on a trip I miss the ever-living hell out of him. When he comes back I can't hug him hard enough and I kiss him all over and tell him that he's never allowed to leave town, or our apartment, ever again.

But when it comes to the Long-Distance Relationship (or LDR) I have a more nuanced opinion. There are two types of LDRs, one that I support and one that I cannot condone.

Together, then apart.

This is the only true long-distance relationship. You've met in person and spent lots of time together and then something terrible happens. One of you has to go to school, gets a job out of town, needs to go back and take care of family, or is in the next season of RuPaul's Drag Race. It is a tough one, but if you are truly in love you will find your own way to weather the distance. For some it involves daily calls and Skyping and constant trips back and forth to see each other. It's painful and expensive, but it's what you have to do so you don't lose your minds and jump off of bridges.

Obviously, you intend to rejoin at a later date and resume the relationship you started before you were torn asunder. Take a deep breath, let loose some sort of battle cry, and do what you need to do. We're all rooting for you. You can do this! If you were truly meant to be together, then this will just be a (terrible) bump in the long romantic road ahead of you.

Apart, then together.

Call me old-fashioned, but I don't believe that a relationship can be started at a distance… an unofficial flirty courtship perhaps. If you haven't been in the same room as one-another and only have a vague concept of when you will ever actually meet and spend time in-person, I do truly believe you are wasting each other's time. I have seen one too many of these silly LDRs in my lifetime. Hell, I was in a few of them myself. They never work out. One guy meets someone closer and that's the end of that, or the two Long Distance Lovebirds finally meet and realize that they had absolutely nothing in common and can hardly stand being around each other for any longer than a ten-minute phone or Facebook conversation.

I'm not saying that it is impossible to meet someone who lives a long way away from you and make something work out. I'm just saying don't file it away as a relationship before you've even begun the due diligence of actually spending time with each other. Don't call each other boyfriends before you've sat in the same physical space for a while. You might feel like you are in a true relationship because of all the phone and online time, but you are only getting tiny snippets of each other–snippets that you can highly control. One of you could be out banging the world and the other would never know about it. You never have to deal with each other's problems or bad moods because you can always just skip a phone call. And let's face it, webcam sex doesn't hold a candle to the real thing.

A commonly held belief is that a Long Distance Relationship is one of the toughest types of relationships that are out there. I disagree. Yes it may feel like your heart is being tugged thousands of miles away and that it hurts like no other possible punishment, but I would like to know if you've ever been in a relationship where you lived with someone. Those are even tougher. You don't have to worry about morning breath and who's walking the dog when you're states apart from each other.

Basically what I'm saying is why put yourself in a long distance situation if you don't have to? Long distance is a massively physically and emotionally challenging handicap to any couple and should only be dealt with when it's introduced. You may be convinced that this person in another time zone is the perfect one for you, but there's probably an absolutely wonderful substitute who would be just as good and he's a lot closer to where you live and work.

How To Melt A Guy's Heart with $2

While we are facing a horrible recession and rampant joblessness we cannot let that hinder romance. So I'm going to give you a recession-minded, fail-safe dating tip. A trick of mine that has proven effective a number of times. It's something you can do fearlessly – it's meaningful and romantic, but not so much so that you'll scare the fella away.

You've started dating a guy and things are going swimmingly. You've been out for meals, drinks, movies, and all of that stuff… but something is missing. You want to romance the pants off of him (literally and figuratively). What do you do?

Buy him something!

Before you cash in your 401k or sell off your television wait up and hear me out. You can actually romance a guy with less than two dollars.

Buy your guy a song.

I don't mean from that guy playing the accordion at the Italian café where you're sharing bruschetta. That's cute too… but it's expected. No, I'm talking iTunes style.

It's safe to say that any guy you might be seeing has an iPod, or iPhone, or Android, or really anything that plays music. I can promise you that chances are high that he has never received a song as a gift. This is because most people don't know that you can actually do this on iTunes. Most people buy gift cards and call it a day.

I have done this about five times to date. Every time the reaction is the same: "Oh my God! You bought me a song! No one has ever done that before!" or "That's the sweetest thing ever! I'm listening to it now!"

The effects are long lasting. Not a month ago I received an email from a guy I dated many years ago. He wanted to see how I was doing and had been thinking about me.

"Why?" I asked.

"That song you bought me came up on shuffle. It really was a sweet gift – do you want to get together for drinks and catch up?"

I'm not kidding. He now associates me with this song.

Originally I would have titled this chapter "How to Melt his Heart with 99 Cents" but iTunes has raised the price on its songs by 30 cents. Trust me, it's still worth it. You don't have to break the bank, it's innovative and technological, and it's not widely done yet.

So here's how you do it:

1. Go on iTunes and find an artist you like that your guy might not know. Pick an Indie band only you know or some folk singer you once heard. No Britney or Beyoncé here boys. Get creative. You must know ONE not-billionaire artist, right? Go with that one. You want something you're sure he's never heard before.

2. On the album page you'll find "Gift This Song" as a dropdown option under the little down-pointing arrow to the right of the track's price. Click that.
3. Fill in the info and in the personal message box write something short like "This song makes me think of you."
4. Click continue and finalize your purchase.
5. Send them a text or IM saying "There's something for you in your email," add a smiley at your own discretion.

Your guy will receive an email and then be taken to iTunes where his song is downloaded for free. Again chances are he didn't know this could be done on iTunes – so there's the initial surprise. Then if you're lucky (or good at picking the right song), the song – its tune, lyrics, message – will speak to him, resonate, and commence melting.

Think of it as this generation's answer to the single red rose and as an added bonus it never dies. Your guy will be shocked, awed, pleased, and hopefully deeply touched. And, in a recession, to get that all for less than two dollars?

It's not being cheap, it's being smart.

Slow Down!

A common mistake that many single boys make is jumping too quickly into a relationship. They have a first date, it works like gangbusters, and they shut down their conversations or flirtations with any other human being they may have been considering dating. They may not be official "boyfriends" yet, but as far as they are convinced it's coming real soon!

This is a bad idea.

Just because you've been on a few dates with a guy does not mean that you are boyfriends. Hell, it doesn't even mean that you are monogamous. You may not be seeing or talking to anyone else thinking that's how this works, but you are wrong. How do you know he's not talking to or hooking up with anyone else? You don't know and if it turns out that he is what can you do about it? "We had that really great date! I assumed we were together!" That only sounds completely and absolutely crazy, doesn't it? Yes it does.

If you halt your dating career every time you meet someone, you are being wildly inefficient. When you're single and dating you need to be a bit more pragmatic. Play the field! Keep yourself open to any possible beau who may come your way. This isn't whorish, slutty, deceitful, or anything of that nature. It's simply the right way to date. We don't grab the first article of clothing when we walk into a store and head straight to the cashier do we? We want to walk around, check a few outfits out, try a few on. We may end up leaving the store having bought nothing. That's okay too.

I am a big believer in going out on many first dates. Every first date you go on will improve your skills and further show you exactly what it is that you want. I also believe that a relationship is not monogamous until it is discussed. Just like your partner should not expect that you are only seeing him you shouldn't expect that of him. This is especially true when you're brand new and just starting to feel each other out.

If you snap directly into monogamy on your second date with someone, you are both doing a massive disservice to each other.

Back in the past when I was single, I would go on dates with different guys every night: a dinner here, a drink there, a walk in the park over there. I silently considered them all in a race with one-another with my heart being the grand prize. I didn't let them know I was seeing other people, nor did they let me know if they were. I didn't care and I don't believe they did either.

I had been dating three guys at once for a few weeks when a clear "winner" pulled ahead of the pack. I found my dates with the other two growing stale. I discovered things about them that just weren't compatible with me. In contrast the third guy and I were naturally spending more and more time together, and the time we spent was getting better and better. He was the winner, and it was time for me to enter into something a little more serious with him so that I could see where we were going. Knowing this I cut off the other two guys, who didn't mind too much because they too noticed that there was no true chemistry there. They were probably seeing other, better candidates as well. I then had the monogamy discussion with the third. I told him that I was interested in only seeing him. He agreed.

A part of you may be screaming out against this approach to dating. It's wrong! My question is simply this: Why? Who says that the second you go on a date with someone that's the only person you should be seeing? That's called a relationship. You are now monogamous boyfriends. Who the hell, besides crazy people, thinks that a boyfriend is made on the first or second date? You don't know each other yet, right? That's why you're dating. And dating is shopping. It is browsing. It is taking a test drive. You don't go to a car lot and drive off with the first SUV you lay your eyes on. Same goes for guys. Relax, and play the field until you hit a Grand Slam.

He's Definitely Not into You

Oh, hey. What's up? Yeah. That's cool. Right. Ok. Yeah. Ha. Huh? Oh. Yeah, definitely. Ah, okay. (silence) (silence) (silence) Oh, sorry I had to do something. Actually I'm out of town this weekend... and busy all week... and morning... and I have brunch with friends....

Now listen, gumshoes! I wish that were a poem or quote from some really angsty indie film (Maybe it is? If not, I claim full copyright).

It's actually a chunk of what I'll call "conTEXT clues." These are signs that the guy you are emailing, IMing, calling, or texting is not whatsoever interested in you.

Now, I am not at all a fan of "giving hints." When I'm not interested in someone, I tell them flat out. And when I am interested in someone, I do the same. However, not everyone is as cool as me (or you if you do the same). Some people play games or are too afraid to just say the truth or just don't care enough about your existence to give you the time of day.

So what you need to do is grab your magnifying glass, look over the texts or responses you're getting, and say "Hmm... is this guy giving me 'hints'?"

If you notice that his texts are often monosyllabic, or responded to days after you sent them or not sent at all, then chances are that you are being given hints and the other guy expects you to disengage. He may not say it right out, but that's what he's saying silently.

Now you may defend yourself and say "He has to be interested! He gave me his number!" This is not an excuse. He could have been drunk, temporarily blind, or just not thinking. These days giving someone your number is about as meaningful as sneezing on them. Just because it's his real number doesn't mean he wants you. Plus people change their minds. They meet better/cuter/richer/funnier guys (or so they think).

If you find the guy you went on a first date with acting this way, I would consider the second date off the table and go back to the drawing board.

First thing you have to do is take a deep breath. This isn't your fault (unless you have been digging through his garbage and he's caught you multiple times).

Next, you have to take action.

How to deal with these clues? Well, there are a few possibilities:

1. **Take the clue and move on.** If you are sure that you're being let down indirectly, you can just simply stop contacting them. If you're anything like me, this may be difficult. I recommend erasing any record of them – phone number, screen name, delete them from your Facebook. It'll stop your itchy, crazy finger.

2. **Confront them.** This is often my preference, and it's fun. Drop him a text or IM and say "Hey, am I bugging you? Are you not interested? Just tell me, it's cool." First of all, you now force the person to be honest and upfront. It's fun watching him squirm. However, I must issue one caution: only do this if you mean it when you say it doesn't matter. If you respond with something bitchy and catty

and filled with expletives and "girl don't even"s, you'll just end up looking like a crazy person.

3. **Continue being clueless.** This one I recommend against, but who am I to tell you what to do? If you want to keep sending out messages into a void of disinterest, it's all up to you. Maybe you have a good data plan and way too much time on your hands. Knock yourself out! The benefit of this is that you will, in time, force the person to be upfront with you and tell you to bug off and leave them alone. Most likely because he doesn't have a good data plan (the fool).

Just remember: It's not you. It's not him. It's both of you. Two people need to be in the right place to make something work. If it doesn't work, it's a shared fault and poor chemistry. Take a deep breath, stop following them on Twitter, and move on with your life. When the situation is reversed and you change your mind about a guy, consider being direct to avoid ridiculousness like this.

Eyes on Me!

I often find myself screaming this on the inside these days while I'm out with guys. We're sitting at a bar, coffee shop, or at a park and talking to each other, and it seems like everything in the world is more interesting than me: a tree, a dog, one of those odd sonnets on the walls of Starbucks.

Why has looking in the eyes of another person fallen so far out of vogue? Is it too much commitment on the first date to look each other in the eyes? If I'm to believe Norman Rockwell paintings as an accurate representation of our history, then as recently as those bygone decades everyone stared moony-eyed at each other for hours at a time over ice cream sodas with two twisty straws. They also wore lots of poodle skirts. We should bring those back.

Then again TV was black and white and the Internet was non-existent back then. Perhaps a face was the most interesting thing you could look at.

I am talking to you so I'm going to look you in the eyes as I do it. I'm going to nod when you speak. For the longest time I viewed this inability to look at a human being as a sign of disinterest. But when the date ended and the guy went in for a kiss or asked me for a repeat, I realized that one thing did not necessarily point to the other.

So then why not look me in the eyes? My best guess is that we are afraid to look into each other's eyes at such an early point in courtship. It is a form of commitment. You are gazing into the soul of the guy across the table from you. What if you show vulnerability? Sadness over an ex you never quite got along with? It's dangerous, but it's also respectful. If you can't look your date in the eye perhaps you need a bit more time in the "single oven."

It's also a way to "play it cool." By not staring at the person you are throwing up a barrier and saying "If you decide I'm not cute or interesting enough for you, it doesn't really matter because that bum soft-shoeing next to that overflowing garbage can on the corner is just as interesting if not more so than you."

May I suggest the following crazy idea? Take the risk. Engage.

Conversely, if it's because you actually do get bored by looking at one thing for too long, you need to balls it up a bit. We are the MTV generation, but we must deal with the fact that our lives are not filled with quick cuts and speedy transitions. We may want to stare into a set of brown eyes, and see a truck exploding, and Zac Efron prancing around shirtless in Cabo, but it ain't happening.

I've never had this problem. Maybe it's so easy for me because I'm a naturally born salesman. Everyone from my grandfather (leading Wear-Ever knife salesman in the US three years in a row in his prime) to my mother and her family has been able to peddle wares to the general populace. So maybe when I look you in the eyes I'm selling something – me, in this case. I want to lock eyes so that you can't get away from me. You have no choice but to engage. I also do it to let you know that I am genuinely interested in what you're saying.

It's also is a great way of connecting with the human who is sharing space with you. You never know what you may see (though you may see them looking at something else.)

Finally, when I go on a date with someone who does look at me as they speak, nods while I talk, etc. they get so many bonus points that they can basically retire as champion by the time we head home. It's rare these days. It's very rare. So if you become one of these rare lookers – your chances of success will soar. If your date's eyes lock onto everything except you, my recommendation is that you silently slink out the door. By the time he remembers to look at you, you'll be somewhere more worth your time.

Title Treatment

So you're seeing someone and it's amazing! You're spending days and nights together. You've got a toothbrush at his place, and he has one at yours. When you're not at one-another's place, you're on the phone like two high school lovers from some sitcom that you can probably catch in reruns on Nick-at-Nite. One night you and your guy are out and about and you crash into a friend. What the fuck do you introduce your guy as? You haven't had the "boyfriend discussion." He may be seeing other guys or you may be seeing other guys because you haven't even had the "Hey, let's not kiss other guys any more... even though we're not technically capital 'B' Boyfriends yet" conversation.

What do you call him?!

It doesn't matter. Call him your guy. Call him by his name and let your friend come to his own conclusions. Call him an alien and tell your friend that his anal probing skills are out of this world.

Titles are completely unimportant in a budding relationship. I don't care if you're dating, fucking, seeing each other, exclusively seeing each other, boyfriends, kinda-boyfriends, or a symbiotic alien pairing. What the world thinks of you is the least important thing that you need to worry about. All that matters is what each of you think of yourselves. The world isn't waking up next to you every morning and dealing with your heinous morning breath before you go brush your teeth; your guy is.

The only time that a title matters is if you think it matters. May I suggest that you not put so much weight on what you refer to yourselves as. Spend more time focusing on getting to know each other, and seeing how a life together might look like down the road.

The more you worry about titles, the more important titles become. That's what makes "Popping The Boyfriend Question" such a stressful point when two guys are going steady. Your stomach twists and you break out in a sweat just to ask him if he's willing to let you put a label on your relationship. Who cares what you're called? The key focus is your relationship. That's what matters.

If you want to have the monogamy conversation to establish that neither of you are seeing other guys go ahead. Don't assume that a "Boyfriend Chat" has any effect on sex or dating or making out with guys when drunk and out at the club. It doesn't.

I feel that a lot of guys put piles of importance on a label for the wrong reason. They assume that slapping the "Boyfriend" label on a guy is the same thing as branding a bull or declawing a cat. You're mine now! You'll never, ever leave me! I can stop looking and self-tanning and get chubby and not worry about my hair so much!

I know you're far too smart to think that securing a Boyfriend Label means that you're set for life, and if you're not smart enough... hopefully now you are.

So if being Boyfriends doesn't protect you from heartbreak or guarantee a happily ever after maybe it's not so important to vigorously pursue the label after all. Have fun! You're dating! Cuddle and kiss and fuck and order Chinese food together when you're drunk. You'll figure out over time what you are, who you are, and what that means.

Don't rush it. Don't push it. Save your labels for the plastic bins where you'll put half of your stuff when one of you moves in with the other.

The Book of Loving

The Cinderella Phase

You wake up next to the man you are going to spend the rest of your life with. You yawn, stretch your arms, and start singing high notes you never knew you were capable of. You jump out of bed in a gorgeous, flowing gown and proceed to dance around the bedroom. Cute, big-eyed woodland creatures come in through the window and proceed to dance and sing along with you!

Welcome to what is commonly known as The Cinderella Phase of a relationship (or the Honeymoon Phase). You made it past the hardest dates and the dates just keep on coming. You've had sex and it was great! The future lies before you and you can see the monogrammed matching bathrobes and towels, the exquisite wedding invitations, your future adorable children. It's okay. I'm not here to burst your balloon. You made it through the wringer of gay dating and may have in fact discovered the perfect guy for you. Enjoy the Cinderella Period. Where everything seems to glisten, glimmer, and gleam. You have a song in your heart and it's always sunny.

But here are some things to keep in mind:

1. **Remember this is a PHASE.** Periods and phases end. They come and go. Do not lead yourself to believe that your relationship will forever be this spectacular, magical, and mystical. I'm not saying you should become cynical. Quite the opposite! This is the honeymoon, baby! Enjoy every last

ounce of the overabundant joy and cheer that you are experiencing, but keep your head on that it could end at any time. And when it does you need to understand that this is because the phase has come to an end, not your relationship.

2. **Don't go missing.** The Cinderella Phase may be lovely for you and your beloved, but it's going to be a huge pain in the ass for your friends and family. You've no doubt noticed that guys in new relationships go missing all the time. Their faces don't end up on milk cartons, but they might as well. A lot of guys fall so hard for the Cinderella Phase that they decide to lock themselves in the bedroom with their new guy and never leave bed. They spend every waking and sleeping moment with their new beau. Their friends and family meanwhile get the shit end of the stick and wonder if they should call the Missing Persons Bureau. Do not make this mistake. Keep your head on just a little. For one you want to keep a bit of independence even when you're just so damn happy. In addition consider the following cynical yet practical reason: if this relationship should end, who will be there for you? Your friends and family will be there. Put in the time with them now so they don't roll their eyes when the first call they receive from you in weeks is a request for free psychotherapy.

3. **Don't be annoying.** Another habit of guys in a Cinderella Phase is broadcasting their absolute happiness continuously day in and day out on social media. Don't do that. Your single friends will not appreciate it. Other people won't appreciate it either. Your happiness is yours. You can share it, but don't over-share it. No one likes a braggart. Remember how you used to feel when you were single and your friends in relationships did

the same thing. You hated it, didn't you? Yes. Yes you did.

4. **Keep your head on.** Cinderella Phases have a habit of lulling us into a state of almost comatose happiness. I urge you to fight this. You want to continue to be perceptive about your relationship, about flaws and issues that might be sneaking around beneath all the joy and sex. Something that may seem small or problematic in Cinderella land may end up being an insurmountable issue once the dumb joy has subsided.

Moving In

So you've been seeing your guy for a long time. You have toothbrushes at each other's apartments. You may even have a designated drawer in each other's bedrooms. Sounds sweet, right? Cute! Adorable. Romantic.

Face it, it's a huge pain in the ass. Inevitably being a couple gets to a point where it becomes ridiculous that you are not cohabiting. Chances are that one of you is the host and the other is the guest. There is rarely a situation where a couple is spending equal time at each other's place. This is not a problem (usually) for the guy who's hosting. It can quickly escalate to a BIG problem for the guy who hasn't laid in his own bed in three weeks.

So, what's the hold up? Why aren't you moving in together? Ah, because you're afraid that this would be moving too fast. Am I right? Of course I'm right. I hear it all the time from guys that I talk to.

My opinion? If you both are wondering if it's time for you to move in together, it's probably time to move in together. Give your poor roommates a break. Take that go-bag your guy has been using and put it in the closet until you go on vacation.

"But wait," you say. "Isn't it too fast? What if it's too fast!?"

Here's the rub: moving in too fast is never the reason that a relationship goes down in flames. Some exes may claim that this is the case, but they are very, very wrong.

Moving In

Moving in with your significant other is basically the same thing as hitting "Fast-forward 100x" on your Netflix or Playstation 4 except it's your relationship not Orange is the New Black.

You go from wanting to see each other when you're not together to always seeing each other and wondering when you'll have time alone. You're the last thing you each see at night and the first thing you see in the morning. You get to share a bathroom and a kitchen and a television. Whereas you previously had the chance to cute-ify yourself prior to seeing one-another, you are now subject to each other at your best and worst. Bed head, bad breath, smelly gas, and all of those things that you did in private are now on full display. Whatever privacy you once had is now out the window. You will hear each other's conversations, see each other's texts, and probably even share the same computer. In other words, you're now in it to win it.

Whether you wait a long time to move in together or do it after a few months, it doesn't matter. The second the lease is signed or the moving trucks have pulled away that fast-forward button has been engaged. Good luck.

If you and your guy are meant to be together, you will move in and continue to be together until you're married and have children. If you and your guy are not meant to be together, your relationship should crash and burn relatively quickly, usually in a matter of months.

I am not telling you this to scare you away from ever moving in with someone. I am actually doing it to get you to relax. If you move in and everything speeds ahead amazingly, congratulations! Enjoy the beautiful gift of splitting your Internet, cable, and utility bills. If your relationship goes down in a belch of flames and screams like the Hindenburg, congratulations! You've just saved yourself years of wasted time ambling along in a relationship that would have self-destructed as soon as you moved in together.

How To Live Together

So you're considering taking the next step with your guy and moving in together? Here's a few tips that I found to work towards keeping a happy home versus one full of broken windows that you've thrown each other out of.

Share and share.

You learned to share in nursery school. Now's the time to really put it into practice. When you are living with a significant other it's best to change everything you once saw as "Mine" to "Ours." This includes computers, stamps, porn site passwords, kitchen stuff, shampoo, and even clothes if you're the same size.

Fair is fair.

If one of you is making more money than the other, I don't think it's a silly proposition that you equitably split your burdens. This covers all bills and expenses that affect each of you equally: Internet, cable, rent, groceries, and utilities. If you make more money than your significant other, consider contributing more to these shared expenses. I'm not advocating that you pay for his dinners out or his Fast Pass or Metrocard, but if you make $100,000 and he makes $40,000, it would be mighty kind of you to pay more towards the rent than he does, don't you agree?

Alone time is okay.

Everyone needs to be alone. We can't stand our parents and siblings all the time. Our co-workers can sure be a huge pain in the ass on Bagel Tuesdays. Even our friends get to be a bit much at certain Sunday brunches. If it's totally okay for us to have time away from all of these important people, why should it be any different for our boyfriends? If you or he needs some time to yourself it doesn't mean that your relationship is about to end and you'll live your life alone. It just means you're two humans in an extremely close vicinity, and sometimes you just need time to yourself.

Maintain your independence.

Sharing your expenses and belongings is one thing. Sharing every human being and social activity can be very, very dangerous. A healthy relationship involves time together and apart, and that time apart doesn't need to be time alone. Keep some friends that you see apart from your live-in hubby. If he goes to Trivia Night once a week with co-workers feel free to join him sometimes, but not always. This produces a two-fold benefit. For one, you will appreciate seeing each other again and have all sorts of things to catch up on. For two, (a much more cynical two) if you and your partner should end up separating, you won't be left floundering without friends or things to do as he returns to his life unscathed.

Respect each other.

This may seem like a "duh" sort of note, but you'd be surprised how often newly moved-in couples might overlook such a simple thing. Respecting your new roommate and his needs is a very important key to lasting together. If he hates messes and you like leaving stacks of dishes in the sink until they congeal into a skyscraper of late-night munchies, perhaps you need to adjust your behavior. If you have to go to bed early one night, it would be nice of him to not have friends over to watch a loud movie or have an impromptu dance party. Simple, but important. Figure out what matters to each of you, and if it's at ends with your behavior or personality. Then adapt or perish.

The Come Down

As I mentioned previously, your amazing Cinderella Phase will inevitably end. What comes next is reality. You've had lots of sex. You've been on tons of dates. You've found out more about each other than you've found out about anyone else you have dated. Now what? Now you stabilize. You come down from the epic high you've been experiencing. Now you get to see if the guy you've been with is everything that you thought he was.

The sad thing is that a lot of guys mistake the end of the Honeymoon Phase as a sign that the "spark" they had is dead. This is why so many young relationships hit the rocks like misguided ships in the dark of night. They claim that the feelings are gone. It's just not the same any more. That they made a terrible mistake. No. Wrong. Your spark hasn't died. You're just finally starting to get to see the real person you've been spending time with.

You may start noticing that you are getting annoyed by things that your partner does. Maybe it's the tone of voice he uses when he's playing video games and you ask him a question. Maybe you're growing sick of a few of his friends. Maybe you've spent so much time together that you both want to go out alone with your friends some night and not just watch another movie on TV. That's okay! It's completely normal. Again do not panic. This is how relationships work. Nothing is new and fabulous forever.

Love is not a magical roller coaster ride that never ends where every minute is a spectacular fantasy. Anyone who tells you that it is has spent far too much time watching Disney movies and not enough time falling in love. True love is the realization that despite the parts of your guy that absolutely drive you crazy, despite the arguments and occasional boredom you may deal with, you still want nothing more than to wake up next to him for the rest of your life.

Now's the make-or-break time boys. Take a look at this real guy you are dating and let him take a long good look at you. He may be a bit different from the Prince Charming you thought you saw when you were flying through the clouds, but that shouldn't be a problem; I doubt you're everything he may have first seen as well.

You're now finally starting to see who your boyfriend really is flaws and all. Is that flawed, actual human being still someone you can't picture waking up without? Yeah? Then continue on, boys. That's true love. It'll only grow stronger and deeper with time.

You Gotta Fight

Arguing is one of the most important parts of being in a long-term committed relationship. Whenever I meet someone who claims that things are completely perfect with his partner and that they never have arguments, I know they are either lying, in a Cinderella Phase, or in a lot of trouble.

You and your boyfriend are two different people. There is no way in hell that all of your wants, needs, opinions, and desires are in perfect alignment. Unless one of you is sacrificing himself for the sake of continuing this charade of an impossibly perfect, argument-free relationship, you should be butting heads on a somewhat regular basis.

Think of your parents or step parents or friends in long-term relationships. I'm sure they squabble with each other pretty regularly. Maybe it's over what directions the GPS gave them when they're in the car, or where they're going for dinner tonight, or what to watch on Netflix, or where the damn house keys went, dammit. This may be annoying to us to watch but it is a perfect example of what a real relationship is.

The cornerstone of a good coupling is open and transparent communication. If you two disagree on something, you better argue about it. State your opinions, have it out, and then move on with your newfound understanding. Now, I'm not telling you to scream at the top of your lungs and slam doors and throw things around. That only happens in movies and bad relationships. Bickering? Yeah, it's pretty natural. It's going to happen. Don't avoid it.

When you and your guy do argue be sure that it is a constructive one and that you're headed to some type of compromise. Don't go into an argument looking for some sort of a decisive "win." This is your boyfriend, not your opponent. The point of your argument should be that you are each trying to get something that you want or need. You should both be prepared to meet somewhere in the middle with both of you giving a little and getting a little.

The worst thing you can do is swallow your feelings and opinions to keep things kosher between you and your guy. It won't work forever. One sad day it'll all come out in something far more explosive and potentially endangering to your relationship than a couple of annoyed grunts about why he can't run to the damn store and buy more toothpaste like you asked him to do ten times.

An important caveat: while arguments should happen in your relationship, they certainly should not be happening every single minute of the day. This could be a sign of something a little more problematic. If you and your boyfriend are not seeing eye-to-eye on anything, perhaps you're not so ideal for each other after all. I cannot tell you what is the "healthy" amount of arguing, but I'm pretty sure that you can figure out when it's too much. If your entire relationship is defined by an escalating number of stand-offs, what's the point of being with him in the first place?

An Open (or) Shut Case

This chapter is going to tackle a potentially divisive subject. I'm okay with that. So, I'm going to talk about Closed (monogamous) and Open (polygamous) relationships. If the very thought of that topic is getting your skin itching and making you consider finding me out one night so you can punch me in the face and blame me for the downfall of gay civilization, do yourself (and my poor, tender, delicate face) a favor and skip ahead to the next chapter.

For those of you who stuck around it's time for some plain talk. I know lots of very happy, very monogamous gay couples. They kiss and sleep with and love only one person and plan to do so until who knows when. I also know lots of very happy, not-very-monogamous couples. I do! It's true. I also know (or have known) a lot of very UNHAPPY monogamous and non-monogamous couples. So needless to say either way you slice this issue you may end up happy, or not-happy.

If you and your partner are 100% monogamous and your sex life is fantastic and all is well, then congratulations! You're monogamous! It's great! Keep up the good work champ! Just put a bookmark on this chapter in case that ever changes.

Now, if you are very happy with your partner and he with you, but one or both of your pairs of eyes is getting a case of wanderlust... don't panic! This does not mean that your relationship is doomed. It simply means that you are men and you have penises. Just because you're in love doesn't mean that you won't be tempted by some hot piece of ass that bounces by you.

What's important is how you deal with wandering eyes. Some guys will simply accept them as a side effect of possessing a penis and continue on happy in their monogamous relationship. That's a fine way to deal with it. There is nothing wrong with that approach. Some other guys, however, can't control their impulses. That's when cheating happens. And the crying. And the screaming. And the fighting. And ultimately the breaking up. And more crying, too.

There is another alternative my friends. It is the Open Relationship. This is not an easy choice to make. Don't expect to open up your relationship and suddenly everything is peachy and you go riding off into the sunset with your boyfriend stopping at the occasional hitching post to do it with some hot cowboy.

Deciding to open up your relationship is only the first of many steps. Allow me to add a quick note: a relationship is very much like a door. As long as you don't rip it off its hinges and turn the wood into pulp it can always be opened and then closed again.

Many people have a predisposed opinion of Open Relationships. The boys in one are not really in love. They're sluts. Why are they even together if they can't keep their dicks to themselves? They should surely break up. This is a very black-and-white judgment, and I hate judgment of any kind.

First off, no open relationship is the same as its brethren. They're like snowflakes or social security numbers. I know a totally monogamous couple here in New York City. They've been together for over twenty years. Once a year they go on vacation for seven days and while they are basking in the sun of Turks and Caicos or Cabo or Miami, they are allowed to sleep with whomever they want, together or apart. They then return to the city and are completely monogamous for the other fifty-one weeks of the year.

I know another couple that is completely monogamous, except for the rule that they are allowed to make out with other guys when they're out and drunk. No sex. No sexual touching. No cuddling. But if one of them is drunk and on a dance floor somewhere? His tongue can hop into any mouth he likes.

I know another couple that only does three ways and only a few a year, but always together. They've been together for ten years and have had no more than ten three ways.

And I know a few open relationships that just do who they want, when they want, where they want, and how they want.

The point I'm trying to make is that open relationships have the potential to be nothing like each other. Monogamous relationships are one thing while open relationships can be anything. Do not take this as a resounding suggestion from me that you open up your relationship. I am merely saying that if everything in your relationship is absolutely amazing except for some human animal urges, throwing the baby out with the bathwater isn't the only option afforded to you. Just because you want to bang some guy really bad doesn't mean you want to wake up with him the next morning and every morning after that.

Abuse is Never Okay

Abuse, either physical or emotional, is never okay in a relationship. I don't care what excuse might slither up from this evil act. It will never be a good enough one.

Couples fight. They fight about everything in the world spanning from who left the toilet seat up to the guy one of them may have been flirting with at the Home Depot. I advocate arguing. It's an important part of a relationship. But these arguments should never devolve into a physical attack or a verbal thrashing.

The day that you or your partner raises a hand or a truly hateful word to the other that relationship is no longer valid. It is over. We do not attack the ones we love. In my opinion we really shouldn't attack anyone or anything, but abuse in a relationship? No way in hell. This isn't a Lifetime Original Movie where the drunkard husband weeps and says "I hurt you because I love you." You never intentionally hurt someone you love. You just don't.

There's no such thing as an accident either. When it comes to abusive relationships Zero Tolerance is the only acceptable approach. It is an unforgivable offense. And if it happens once I guarantee you that it will happen again. No matter how hard you believe your guy didn't mean it, or was in a crazy place, or whatever, he will do it again. He will do it over and over again. And the longer you excuse him, the more codependent you will become. This will not end well.

Get the hell out. Now. If you need to call the cops or a helpline, do it. Right now. Tell your friends or family. Tell authorities. Run. Do not believe him when he has an excuse. Do not give him an excuse he can use. There is never a good reason to raise a hand to your partner and there never will be.

And if you are the one who has considered abusing your partner, I recommend that you also seek counseling. This is a completely inexcusable thing to do and you need to deal with it sooner rather than later. Get help and get it fast. Your actions could have very serious legal and social consequences.

The Book of Breaking Up

When It's (Possibly) Time to Break Up

Breaking up is sadly a significant part of many relationships. A quick glance at our nation's divorce rates or all the breakup notifications on your Facebook newsfeed should be all the evidence you need to ascertain that. To go into a relationship and expect it to last forever is a hopeful mentality, but it may not be completely accurate. You need to be comfortable with the notion of breaking up–because settling for something that's substandard just because you don't want to be alone is both stupid and self-destructive.

When Do You Break Up? This is a crucial decision. Naturally when we enter into a union with a guy, we imagine it lasting forever. We get married on the beach, wake up every morning to breakfast in bed, and sing with cute forest creatures while we do our chores. Of course that doesn't always happen. So when do you know you should break up? Here are some good signs:

1. It's only been a short time and you ALREADY have problems.

Heed these words carefully: All relationships should come with a Honeymoon period. It's where your partner is everything to you and your eyes are fluttering and you kiss and peck and Skype with each other every night. Your Facebook friends want to murder you because all you do is call each other "Kissy" on each other's walls, post pics of you kissing, and throw Hershey's Kisses at each other.

It won't last forever, so enjoy it!

If, however, you don't get that Honeymoon period and are already fighting within a few days or weeks of dating... that's serious evidence that maybe this isn't what you're looking for. Everyone is entitled to a Honeymoon. If you're getting screwed in that department, ask yourself the golden question: why? If you're already incompatible and not getting along what does the future hold?

Relationships get tougher over time, not easier. It's the physics of love. So if you're starting in a bad place maybe you should go start in a different place with a different guy.

2. They don't give you what you want even after you ask.

Do you need to be texted when your boyfriend is going to be coming home late? Do you want your beau to ask you about your day when you get back from work? Are you expecting sex in the morning, afternoon, and/or night? Does he need to go out with you or stay in with you on certain nights?

You have every right to have expectations of your relationship primarily because we go into relationships to make ourselves happier and complete ourselves. And your partner has every right to deny your request... because he's looking for happiness too. That's compatibility folks.

If you feel something is lacking, tell your partner about it. Talk to him. Don't play games. Come right out and say what you want, let him tell you what he wants, and come to a consensus (i. e. you give a little and he gives a little). If that happens and your partner still doesn't fix it, it may be grounds for breaking up. You're just not compatible.

3. You catch them lying.

Lying is a big deal in relationships. Boyfriends need to be able to trust each other. Yes, the average human being tells up to twenty lies a day but they tend to be white lies, also known as lies that keep the world moving and peoples' feelings intact.

If you catch your boyfriend lying to you multiple times, it may be time to split up. First and foremost, talk to him. Tell him that transparency is important. That you'd rather know than not know. If it continues… get outta there. You need to build trust, not walk around living in a world of doubt all the time.

4. Your eyes wander TOO much.

Do you find yourself wanting to bone every hot guy you pass? Well, that's still pretty natural. We're sexual beings. Seeing a gorgeous guy will almost always grab our attention. A relationship is not a blindfold. We still have penises.

However, if that attraction gets more tempting, if you feel like you're missing out or not living it up or just want to hop in a few more beds, it may be time to take a trip to Splitsville. Maybe you're not ready to settle down just yet.

A disclaimer: this really only matters for recent relationships. I believe that all relationships should start with monogamy. You need a baseline to start from.

If you and your partner have been together for years and your eyes start wandering, I advocate some serious conversations. Perhaps you can open up your relationship a little bit? It's difficult. It may not work. If your sex life is awesome, your relationship is awesome, and your love is strong and all you are dealing with is a bit of excess testosterone and bonering... it may be worth talking over.

5. The sex sucks.

Sex is important. Scratch that, it is very important. If the fornicating you're getting isn't worth the fornicating you're giving, it's time to hightail it.

Are you both stubborn tops? That's bad. The same result for strict bottoms. Simple sexual compatibility is very, very important. But what about when the issue is more... complex?

It's all about communication. Each of us is hardwired a different way sexually. Unfortunately we don't come with Fuck Manuals. If you want something of your partner you must tell him. Do you want them to slap you around? Maybe you want to rim him. Maybe you want to role play, or focus more on the nipples, or not shower after the gym.

If you know what gets you going be sure to let them know. Otherwise you can't possibly hold them responsible for not meeting your needs. No one's a Sex Psychic.

How To Break Up

So you have come to the end of this road. You have decided that it's time for your beau to go… now how do you make the cut? This isn't Project Runway or Drag Race. You can't just drop a catch phrase and cut to the scene of them packing their knives in the Top Chef kitchen. It requires more work. Unpleasant work? Nay, shitty work. But guess what? If you are doing the breaking up, you need to expect it to be dirty like slitting the throat of a chicken.

Here are a few tips for when it comes to the breakup:

1. It's never the "RIGHT" time.

Basically what I mean by this is don't be a coward. It will simply never be a good day to break up with someone. Similar to the fact it's never a good day to get kicked in the balls. No matter when you break up with someone, he will always have something to say about the day you did it. He broke up with me on my birthday! On Valentine's Day! A day before Valentine's Day! Two weeks after Valentine's Day! On the anniversary of my dog's death!

Honestly no one ever thinks of breaking up with someone on Valentine's Day. You were probably thinking about doing it for a long-ass time and finally couldn't take it anymore. Once you've decided to break up with someone, do the both of you a favor and get it over with.

2. Be the asshole.

If you're breaking up with someone, you are always going to be the asshole. To make it as clean as possible it is best to take all of the responsibility on yourself. It's your fault. You're the bag of dicks. You thought he was the one, and then you changed your mind. You're a depraved scumbag and a liar and you're so sorry you unleashed this horror on him.

It doesn't matter if your soon-to-be-ex is actually the asshole (or equal parts asshole). A breakup is a tiny bit easier when you steal his thunder, admit you're a dickface, and nod silently and sullenly as they repeat to you how much of a dickface you are. Because in the end who cares if he thinks you're an asshole? You're off to get laid by your second-most recent ex tonight.

3. Do it in person (or over the phone).

Only do it over the phone if you're far, far away from each other. Otherwise do it in person. Never break up with someone via Facebook or text or smoke signal. Reason one not to do this: because it's shitty. Reason two not to do this: because there is now permanent proof on a social network, or your ex's phone, that you are a cockschmuck of the highest degree. Trust me, he will show everyone. And because you were too afraid to confront your ex-guy face-to-face, there goes your reputation.

Break ups are supposed to be hard and uncomfortable. Stop trying to make them peaceful and rosy... it won't work. You owe the dumpee at least some respect. You also need to let him express his own feelings of anger/sadness/righteousness/whatever. It's just the human thing to do.

4. Don't say why.

When you break up with someone his first desperate clinging maneuver is to ask you why. Let me tell you right now: no matter how logical, realistic, honest, or simple your answer is, it will never be a good enough answer. If you're firm in your decision to end this, then end it. Don't tell them why.

If you must tell them why, tell them that you just can't. It's not what you wanted. You're not ready for something this serious right now (which is key, just in case you act like an idiot and start dating someone else two days later).

Unfortunately, guess what? All those answers are bullshit too. Who knows why you're breaking up with him? Well, you do. And that answer may range anywhere from I met a hotter guy to I just wanna be slutty to I can't stand how high-pitched your voice is to any old thing. The reason doesn't matter. What matters is that it's over. Don't belabor it.

5. Plead the fifth.

Once you have broken up with your ex, it is your job to shut the fuck up about him. Don't start walking around town saying how small his dick is or how bad the acne on his back was. That's double shitty. Remember the humbling fact that you already broke his heart.

I don't care what your ex says about you. When you hear it second-hand shake your head, cluck your tongue, and say something like "I feel so bad I hurt him like that. He sounds really angry. I hope he can get over it soon." Why? Because he is destroyed and he is angry. You might be too, but say nothing about him. It's time to move on.

How to Get Dumped

Let's not bother with why he did it or how much you didn't deserve it. Let's put aside your feelings for a second and all the countless times you'll be revisiting the moment he told you "we're through," as well as temporarily forgetting the many, many happy and complex moments you shared before.

What's important is the following fact: you've been dumped.

What do you do now? Well in my opinion, there are a few ways to go about this.

Disclaimer: All of these suggestions assume that he is legitimately through with you. If you truly, truly believe that he's going to come back, then Godspeed. Go back and get that guy!

For the rest of you, or those of you who felt the way I described in the last paragraph, chased him, got shot down, and came back to this chapter… let us begin:

1. Cut him off.

This is of course the cleanest way to go about a post-breakup situation. He is dead to you. Unfriend him on Facebook. Delete his phone number. Set everything he ever got you on fire. Cut off his friends who weren't originally your friends. Beg your friends who weren't originally his friends to cut him off similarly.

While this is the cleanest option it's also the most difficult to pull off. You will find yourself doubting the choice you made. You'll find him going crazy and trying to get you back. Or maybe you're one of the few people who can cut him loose like a hangnail and move on. If so, congrats! You're a better man than I.

2. Push him to the limit.

Oh shit. You did that horrible "Let's totes be friends!" thing. NOOOOO! Why did you do that? Why would you ever do that? That's the worst possible thing that you could do. I myself have done this no less than ten times in my dating career. And without doubt I'm sure I'd do it again in a heartbeat despite the fact I'm telling you right here not to do it.

So now you're stuck occasionally texting him. Sometimes you're calling him. Sometimes you're working out with him. And you're all smiles and "Howdy-do's"… until he leaves and you explode in tears and punch your pillows until the stuffing flies out.

It's time to push him to the limit. Chances are every time you get a fresh dose of searing love-pain, you pull back from him. You delete him on Facebook only to later add him again. You delete his phone number, but have it written down on a card somewhere. You find ways to crash into him when you're out.

Go ahead and keep this tomfoolery up. You can't cut him off and so now it's his job to do the cutting. I assure you, soon enough he won't be able to deal with your flip-flopping flim-flammery. He'll cut you off for good, you'll experience the heartbreak you've been avoiding, and life will go on.

3. Engage your Kill Switch.

I believe that inside each of us there is a time and pain-sensitive Kill Switch. The period of time and the threshold of pain for activation varies. But when you reach a certain consecutive period of god-awful heartbreak, the switch will throw and you'll... suddenly... feel... nothing.

I know this switch well because it's happened to me many times. One day you'll roll out of bed having not slept more than five minutes the night previous. You'll go to the bathroom and jump in the shower. You'll step out and, lo and behold, find yourself thinking of something else. Whether it's pizza, another cute guy, or a friend you haven't called in a while, it'll be a complete change in mental direction for you.

At first you may be tentative. Is that really it? Are you over him? Did it really happen that suddenly? Yes. We can only suffer for so long.

So what does all of this mean? It means no matter what path you take, sooner or later you will be over him. This is to comfort you when all those friends you repeat your woes to day in and day out finally throw up their hands in frustration. Anyone who tells you to "just cut him off" doesn't get it. That's fine. That's why he or she is most likely never going to be a couple's counselor.

You have a right to your pain and heartbreak. You have a right to try and get over him in any way you can (so long as he isn't physically hurt in the process). It'll be rough. It'll suck. You'll cry a lot. You might puke or lose twenty pounds from not eating.

Breakups are messy and they suck. Just rest assured that one day, whether he cuts you off, you cut him off, or you cut yourself loose from him, you will be free. You will move on.

How to Get Over Him

Here's the thing about break-ups: Everybody hurts. (Thank you, R. E. M.) Whether you're the guy who cuts it off or who gets the cut, you both will ultimately feel the sense of loss at one time or another. Whether it's a fresh wound right after the ending or a delayed response weeks later when you're drunk and realize you may have just given up your one, true shot at happiness, you will feel it.

Here's the thing. Time heals all wounds. What seems like the end of the world and your final chance at happiness now will be nothing but a faded memory down the line. How long down the line? Well I don't know. Everyone processes these things differently. Eventually you will see that this is indeed true.

The guys that broke my heart ten years ago have either completely disappeared from my life or are now some of my greatest friends. I have been a guest at ex-boyfriends' weddings. I still grab brunch or drinks with guys I swore, at the time, that I would never forgive nor ever acknowledge ever again.

So take that tidbit of info and tuck it away in your pocket. It may not be a major comfort to you, but I'm not here to give you comfort. I'm here to tell you how it's going to be.

Let me give you some permission right here. I give you the permission to grieve. You have every right and freedom to be as miserable, angry, depressed, jealous, or destroyed as you feel. In fact, it's sort of a pre-requisite to getting past the pain.

Think of the pain from a break-up like a stomach full of too much vodka. You can try to ignore the roiling and gurgling but it's going to have to come out. Same with your feelings. The more you try to "feel better" or "get past" the feelings, the worse they will get for you. You have been through a terrible, heart-breaking ordeal. How could you possibly feel good about what has happened? This isn't a quick one-and-done-type thing. So let it out.

Tell your friends, or your family, or a psychologist, or a social worker. Give yourself the permission to cry and punch your pillow and have sleepless nights and curse the gods in the heavens above. Every time you do it you're that much closer to getting the heartbreak vodka out. This won't be easy. It won't be quick. But I can tell you this from personal experience: in time, it will go away. Even when you look and see nothing but darkness ahead of you, listen to someone who's been in the darkness before. In time it goes. It always does. It always will.

The Book of Doing It

Safe Vs. Stupid

There are few things that I consider in black and white terms. Safe sex is one of them. When you go out into the world, meet someone, go home with them, and take part of them or give them a part of you, a condom is not a question. It is an absolute requirement.

There is a new movement called pRep (where you take anti-HIV drugs prior to infection to help stave off infection), but even this does not excuse the use of condoms. STDs and STIs are very much a part of our reality. And unless you want an excuse to go to your friendly neighborhood clinic, wrap it up and keep it that way.

I don't care if he told you he's clean. I don't care if he says he's undetectable. I don't care if you're clean or you're undetectable. You wouldn't let a doctor put a used syringe in your arm to take your blood. Why would you let someone put something they've used a ton of times inside of you, or vice-versa? You wouldn't.

Safe sex is a reality that we all must come to accept. Sure, it may not feel as good. Maybe it makes your orgasm harder to achieve. Deal with it. Put on a condom. No excuse you could possibly have for skipping a condom is a good one.

Recently I was speaking with someone who was considering having bareback sex with a guy he had met. He told me that the guy said he was clean but that he could only get aroused if he wasn't wearing a condom. My response to the boy was very simple: "Do you think you're the first person that he's said that to? How many other guys has he slept with without using protection? Don't be stupid."

I actually know a lot of guys who won't even have protected sex with someone once they hear that the guy has an STD or an STI. If you're one of those people, it makes you an absolute hypocrite to have unprotected sex. Are you simply assuming that everyone you're sleeping with is STD/STI-free?

Don't be silly. Please don't.

Gay Sex 101

Before I get into the nitty-gritty of gay sex, I wanted to get some basic knowledge across to you. We'll go deeper, and harder soon. I promise. But first...

Why so serious?

Sex is a crazy thing. It's silly. It's weird. It's funny. It's awkward. I suggest that you embrace this reality before you rip off each other's clothing. We as humans are complex machines with tons of working parts. There will be gurgles and squishes and smells and all matters of mistakes, foibles, fumbles, and bumbles. Clothing is tough to take off. We have gag reflexes. Some peoples' bodies turn beet red when they're about to orgasm. Some guys need to pinch their nipples and massage their taints to get themselves over the edge. My secret? Have fun with it. You don't need to bite your lip and pretend you're some porn star. Laugh, giggle, and understand that sex is a lot more awkward of a thing than any of us would ever care to admit.

Porn isn't reality.

Anyone who goes into a sexual encounter expecting to replicate something they've seen in gay porn is setting themselves up for a metric ton of disappointment. By its very design porn is as phony as sex can get. A twenty-minute gay porn scene most likely took six to eight hours to shoot. The actors got tons of breaks to take a Viagra, watch some of their own porn, get some water, have makeup reapplied, and lighting fixed. They're not always actually penetrating each other. Sometimes they even use stunt butts if the bottom isn't ready to go or the dick is too big. Hell, they have a director behind the camera telling them what to do and how to do it and an editing team that cuts hours and hours of footage into a visually riveting twenty-minute, masturbatory masterpiece. Real sex is not porn sex, and it never will be. And anyone who told you they had porn sex is either lying, was drunk, or watches really boring porn.

Don't be selfish.

You should enter into a sexual encounter with one goal: pleasuring your partner. This is very much like the rule of Karma: the more positive energy you put out into the world, the more positive energy that comes flying back at you. If you pleasure the pants off of your partner, he'll be likewise encouraged to go above and beyond to bring you pleasure. Conversely, if either of you is entering into the act looking just to get your rocks off, you'll probably miss out on a ton of fun.

Communicate, communicate, communicate.

So many of us have been so conditioned by hours of porn watching that we feel awkward when we get to have our own, actual sex. It feels weird to tell someone to do something or not do something. We don't know that we can ask questions and that either a yes or no answer is totally okay. We just make some noises, whisper stupidly so we can sound porn-sexy, and stumble through the act in a way that isn't half as good as it ultimately can be. So speak up friends. Ask questions. Make suggestions. Be comfortable saying no or yes.

Flip flop!

Once upon a time gay men proudly self-identified as either total tops or total bottoms. That is no longer the case whatsoever. More and more guys have become allergic to the idea of a sexual label and are bouncing all along the spectrum of giving and taking. More often than not you may very well find yourself with a truly versatile guy. What does this mean? Flip flop! Take turns on each other. Switch from pitcher to catcher. The experience will be even more exciting and interesting with you both having your cake and eating it too.

Top Tactics

So you're a Top. Maybe you're verse but you're in a topping mood or you're usually a bottom, but the guy you are getting it on with simply refuses to stick it in you. There are a number of tactics and tips in this chapter to help you give, and get, the best possible sexual experience:

The bottom's The Boss.

You may be the dominating half of the coupling in question, but only in the sense that you are entering him. Remember that the bottom is actually the boss. He calls the shots. He gets to state the rules. Why? Because if you piss him off, your dick gets stuck out in the cold with no way back inside. You won't even be invited to his annual Christmas party. Don't fuck it up fellas.

Ask first.

Perhaps the bottom isn't in the mood to take you inside tonight. This might end up being a strictly oral evening. This is ok! Do him a courtesy and ask him to let you inside before you make a move for the condom or his legs. If you're lucky, he may just ask you right out which makes the whole penetration dance even easier.

Keep communicating.

Sure, we've seen pornos where the top or bottom is all "Oooh yeah, you like that bitch? You like when I X and Y your Z? Yeaaaaah." I'm not talking this sort of communication. As a good top you should be in constant communication with your partner. Find out what he likes and what he doesn't like. The more he likes what you're doing to him, the more you'll like what he does back to you.

Lotsa lube.

Do you think your dick is slick enough? Put a few more generous dollops on top bud. On the whole, most tops never really get the amount of lube required right. This results in friction, which results in pain, which results in the bottom shutting down. Lube him up, inside and out, and then dump the rest of the bottle all over your dick. There's no such thing as too much lube where body parts are concerned (furniture and upholstery is a totally different story).

Start slow.

Very few bottoms appreciate you slamming yourself in to the hilt without a warning shot. It's a shock to the system, and not the pleasurable kind of shock. Whether you're with a proud power bottom or a relative newbie, every bottom appreciates a good warm up. Start with a finger or your tongue and then move forward from there. Take it slow until they invite you to move faster. Don't worry, they will. If they don't, it's good that you hesitated because that would've ended with them yanking you out and slamming the door.

Keep it in.

It may be really hot in porn when that big, buff top shoves himself all the way inside, pulls himself all the way out, and then fires himself right back in again. Turns out this is not the most popular thing among many bottoms. Stick it in and keep it in. If he's one of the bottoms that appreciates that sort of thing, he'll let you know.

Switch it up!

Please don't be a boring top. Have more tricks up your sleeve than a monotonous and boring "thunk-thunk-thunk." That's not fun. The bottom might even fall asleep. Switch your thrusting speed up. Go fast then go slow. Go all the way in and squeeze your kegels to make your dick a little thicker, then do some mini thrusts while you're still inside. My point is simple but vital: be creative. Just because you're inside of him doesn't mean that your job stops there.

It's all about angles.

If you've had enough sex with enough guys, you've surely discovered that dicks come in different shapes and sizes. On the flip side of the sex-coin the inside of a bottom comes in pretty much one model. Whether you curve up or down or left or right or are straight and narrow, work with the bottom to find the angle and position that allows you inside the easiest with the least amount of discomfort for him. It may take a few tries, but you'll find something that fits and it's smooth sailing from there.

Reach around.

Don't just plunge relentlessly into your partner and let his dick swing to and fro like a cowbell. Take a hold of that thing and work him with one of your free hands. If you can get him into a crazy position that allows you to blow him while topping him, he may very well thank you with a second round later on.

Shit happens.

So you're going at it, but then you hear some sounds and notice some scents. It happens. Sometimes the "cave of wonders" sends you back a gift you never asked for. That's okay. Take a break. If the bottom is embarrassed, try not to make him feel any worse. Hell, take him with you into the shower to clean up. You can always try for round two.

Cleanliness counts.

The bottom isn't the only guy who's supposed to keep up on his body hygiene. Be sure to shower and trim and deodorize before you take it into bed. No one wants to bed down with a slob. This can be completely thrown out the window if the guy you're with wants you ripe and/or bushy. In that case skip the shower and off you go. But if you're dealing with a new partner, do them the courtesy of bathing and up-keeping.

Eye contact.

You need to understand that penetration is a very intimate act for a bottom. It should also be very intimate for you, but there's something about surrendering yourself to someone else and allowing them to enter you that really takes it out of you. Give your partner the respect of eye contact. Give him a smile or two. Don't just treat him like a piece of meat or a living sex toy. Unless he asks for you to do just that.

Best Bottom Behavior

First off, allow me to give you my personal thanks and appreciation for the good work you are doing. One of the worst things I see and hear is when tops walk around saying they're "the real men" in the gay world. You know better. You're the one who deals with pain and mines pleasure out of it. You have the truest sense of ecstasy from sex. Without you, tops would be sticking their dicks in wall sockets and apple pies to get off. You are doing the Lord's work. Do not think for a second that your valor and hard work are going unrecognized.

Now here are some tips and tactics if you are only just recently getting into the bottoming scene:

Relax!

Being comfortable during sex is the absolutely most important thing that should be on your mind before you bottom. Stress, discomfort, worry, fear, or any other sort of negative emotion or feeling can make the sex a lot less enjoyable for you literally causing you to tighten up. I do not recommend the use of alcohol or drugs to achieve this relaxation. I am sure that many others would disagree with me. Either way take a deep breath! You're about to have a ton of fun with a guy you want to be with. If for some reason you cannot relax, perhaps bottoming shouldn't be on the menu tonight. Your comfort is key, or neither of you will enjoy the night.

Cleanliness is godliness.

This is an honest fact: you can just lie there, checking your Facebook while the top goes to town on you yawning the whole time and he'd have a blast. Obviously I don't advocate you doing that, but it's true. You're about to take something in reverse up your butt, which is a zone that's much more often used for taking things out of your body. Unfortunately a thorough shower is not really going to do the trick. Invest in douche or an enema system and keep it at your home. On a night when you anticipate that you are going to get it on, give yourself a good, thorough cleansing. Be sure to wait at least forty-five minutes after you clean out before you take something inside of you. This way you can guarantee that you won't experience the surprise "second wave."

Don't just lie there.

While you could just lie there and take it like a champ, why would you? Sex is a lot more fun and memorable when both partners are going at it full-force. Hop on the top and take a ride. If you're going doggy, back up on it. Suggest a position change. Grab the back of his ass and pull him in deeper. Have fun! If you just wanted to lie around, why did you bother letting a sweaty dude jump all up inside of you in the first place?

Let your voice be heard.

You might be surprised that a lot of tops are actually very sensitive and anxious. Whether because they've had very little experience or they've had bad experiences, they aren't giving you all they've got. The top might not always be able to communicate that they want to go farther, deeper, or harder. So let your partner know. If you want it a certain way, or you want them to take full control, or you want them to slow down, just make sure you let them know. I guarantee you they'll be very receptive to your recommendations.

Don't be the hero.

The top isn't a mind reader. Let him know if what he's doing is uncomfortable or painful to you. Most tops want to make you feel as good as you're making them feel, and have no interest in bringing you unwanted pain or displeasure. Tell him to slow down, tell him to be gentler, or tell him you need to take a break. You have every single bit as much of a right to enjoying yourself as he does. So be sure you're looking out for you.

Take control!

Dominance and submission is so last year. If you want to surprise a top and give him a night he'll never forget, take control and show him what you're made of. Push and pull him around. Tell him to do what you want him to do. Blow his mind and match his force and activity with an equal ration of your own.

Hole health.

This is a message for those proud power bottoms out there. Bear in mind that your butthole, sphincter, and rectum aren't made out of titanium steel. They do stretch. They can tear. All sorts of terrible horrible things can happen to you years down the road due to disrespecting your man apparatus. I'm not telling you this to scare you. I'm just saying if you had a really expensive computer would you bang the keyboard, mouse, and screen with your fists? No, you'd take a bit better care of it. Your hole health is important. Keep that in mind.

One Night Only

Everyone has had a one-night stand at some point in their lives. If you know someone who says they never have, they are lying to you. Whether we knew that the one-night stand was going to be a one night only or we were misled into believing that there would be a longer timeline to the carnal courtship, every single one of us has found ourselves in a guy's bed that we would never see again.

If you think about it, all sexual encounters start off as a one-night stand. It's then up to the two (or more) participants if the interaction will upgrade to a multiple-night stand or a relationship.

I am a very strong advocate of sex even for guys who are "just looking" for a meaningful, monogamous relationship. Why? Because sexual compatibility is an integral part of any relationship. If you're not good together naked, you've just knocked out a significant part of your relationship.

So go out there and have your sex. Be safe about it. And try not to be too upset if that one night ends up being the only night.

If you enter willingly into a one-night stand, here are some things to keep in mind:

To host or not to host?

When I was singling and mingling, I would always host. This was mostly because I liked my apartment and I couldn't sleep in a stranger's bed. I also had a habit of picking up guys who lived rather far away while my apartment was only a quick ten dollar cab. There are risks and rewards with either end of the hosting coin. If you host, this person now knows where you live. He could rob you while you're asleep (I've heard stories). If you have roommates, they might hate you the following morning. The pro of this arrangement is that you don't have to deal with a walk of shame in the morning. If you go home with another guy, you are now in his control. If he takes you far away from home, you could very well be stuck there if things go south. You also don't know the state of his place or who he's living with. It's risky but if you can't host, you may have no other alternative. Either way just be safe and smart when you get in the car or subway or train or bus.

Know what you're getting into.

There are a few questions you are very much allowed to ask before you seal the deal and leave for a one-nighter. Find out if he's a top or a bottom. Nail him down to whether he has a boyfriend or not. You can grill him on his STD/STI status. You can make sure that you're just going to be sleeping with him and he doesn't have a boyfriend or roommate at home waiting for you. Also, you can (and should) establish before you walk out the door that this will be a safe sex endeavor. If any of the answers are not what you're looking for, you've saved yourself from a wasted night and can go back on the hunt.

Get to it.

When you go home with a guy, there should be no doubt what you are there for. This isn't like some coming-of-age gay movie where you sit around having awkward conversations or giving each other massages until a spark happens. As soon as you get into the house, apartment, or room, just get it started. I assure you that no one will be surprised or have a problem with your speed. Chances are that the hour is late and you both have something to do the next morning.

After the fact.

When the sex is done and your loads are blown... what next? I advocate a good laugh and an immediate pivot into conversation. Chances are you haven't spoken much before you came home and you want this to be a smooth transition. Sex compliments are good. Eventually the ultimate decision arrives:

Stay over or get out?

It's post-coitus. You're lying in a sweaty heap on the bed or kitchen floor. Now what? Do you get suited up and return to the real world to battle the sun and the judgmental roommates/dormmates/doorman of your one-nighter? Do you cuddle up and pass out beside him? This decision is usually a two-step process, offer and acceptance. If you're the host, you ultimately decide whether staying over is an available option. If you're not the host, you have the right of refusal if they invite you to stay.

Friends with Benefits (or Detriments)

When I was younger I thought that Friends with Benefits sounded like a nonsensical idea. How could I spend that much time with someone in such an intimate way and then not end up being boyfriends? Impossible! Then I ended up in a Friends with Benefits relationship. I was proven right.

I am not a believer in Friends with Benefits. While it may seem like a heaven-on-earth arrangement, it's usually a terrible situation for one of the guys involved. I don't care what you say about how you feel; the more time you spend sleeping with someone, the more of a connection you will forge with them. One of you will inevitably end up jealous, in love, or who knows what.

Then again, I know a fair number of couples that kicked off their courtship as Friends with Benefits. Why is this? It is because of the fear of labels that I discussed earlier in this book. We are so afraid of commitment or even the concept of commitment that we are willing to pretend we're just friends who get naked with no serious discussions in order to avoid the serious questions.

All Friends with Benefits relationships end. If you enter into one be prepared for this and understand what it means. You and your friend are fucking. You are not boyfriends. You are not committed to each other in any physical or emotional way. If one of you finds a guy that you like, you will inevitably have to stop fucking once that outside relationship gets serious. This seems like an okay thing until you're the guy who no longer has a beneficial friend. When that happens you'll ultimately feel like shit because your Friend with Benefits saw something more in this new guy he's with that you apparently didn't have. This is not a good feeling to experience. To add to the drama, your friend will not be able to confide in you about his new relationship because you are no longer an impartial party.

From what I've seen, one of the guys in a Fuck Buddy arrangement usually feels a lot more than he's letting on. He has feelings for his Fuck Buddy but can't express them, or he has expressed them and the other partner simply isn't interested. Friends with Benefits tends to more often be one Friend with Benefits and the Other Friend Being Upset But Playing Along.

Friends with Benefits has the ability to ruin a lot of real friendships. If you think you have a chance of something more with a friend, bet the house and ask them out. Doing a Friends with Benefits arrangement is more volatile and doesn't promise anything besides some temporary ass.

A FWB arrangement is a very risky relationship. It is more risky than just dating each other and getting it over with. It is more romantically risky than one-night standing your way across the globe. You will certainly end up forming an attachment to each other, which will only complicate matters because you're just supposed to be getting it on for fun so you don't have to bother with boyfriends!

I'm not saying ban yourself from these types of relationships. I just want to make sure you know the risks involved so that I can say "I told you so" when it blows up in your face.

Here are the takeaways you need to remember:

1. The Friends With Benefits relationship always ends. Either in a sudden halt of all sexual activity or in a romantic coupling.

2. Once the benefits go away, the friendship probably will too. We can tell our friends about hot sex we're having or relationship problems we're dealing with, but how could you tell a former Fuck Buddy about sex you're having with someone that is no longer him?

3. If your FWB situation continues even after one of you gets into a relationship, you have a whole new host of problems that must inevitably be dealt with… including a poor sucker who's dating one of you and is none the wiser about what you are doing.

4. FWB sex should always be safe. You may be lulled into believing you can eschew safety because you are regular partners, but by the very doctrine of your coupling you are both allowed to sleep with whomever you want.

Approach this with caution friends. Friends with Benefits may seem like a good idea, but it rarely ends up that way. Understand the risks and know that you're playing with fire.

Three, Four, or More

One on one is plenty of fun, but sometimes it's just not enough. What happens when you want to add a few extras into the mix? Here are a few tips:

You need a director.

Who's bottoming? Who's topping? Will this just be an oral outing? Out loud communication is the best tip I can give for any scenario. Sure, on porn they just seamlessly switch from position to position. Everything works out perfectly. That's because there's a director behind the camera who's pre-planned and run through the entire scene in advance. They get to take breaks to pee and clean out and maybe get some Gatorade. You don't have the benefit of a well-paid director or porn union rules. So don't try to emulate porn when doing the group thing. It won't work. It'll be awkward.

These situations work out best when one member volunteers as "the director." He's the guy who tells everyone else what to do. Odds are the other members have never done this before or have no experience with each other and will be thankful for some friendly instruction.

Threeways.

Ah, the magical Threeway. The most popular section of scenes on any gay porn (or straight!) website. A horny hat trick. A carnal pile of guys reduced to their truest animal instincts. More often than not, threeways are not about love or commitment. They're about a bunch of very hot and bothered guys crumbling all over each other in a truly explosive concoction of humanity.

Thing is threeways are a lot more difficult to pull off than they look. If you've been in one, you'll know this is a fact. If all you have to base your understanding on are a few scenes you've seen or stories you've heard, you have a lot to learn.

The threeway situation is a complex one. The first thing to consider is obvious: who are the members? Are two a couple and a third's a guest? Is it three complete randoms coming together? Is it three friends after a night of too much drinking? Maybe it's two friends and a random. For a situation only involving three people there are numerous combinations that can completely change the make-up of the making out.

Don't head into a threeway if you are not attracted to both of the guys. In a sexual situation where there are more than three playing, this is a different story, but a threeway is still a fragile, intimate, personal grouping. If one member feels left out, the whole thing could explode in a very awkward and un-sexy way. You may really, really want one member and think that you are willing to deal with the other, but it will not work out.

For couples, a threeway is best seen as you two allowing a guest in. He is your focus. He is your plaything. Team up together to take him on. This can help to push off any awkward feelings of jealousy that can arise when a couple brings in someone else who might be more interested in one of them than the other. If you're both taking him on, he won't have the chance to make a choice.

If you are brought into a threeway with a couple, I ask that you be equitable and act as though you are equally attracted to both of them even if you are not. Why? Because if you don't treat them fairly you could create a lot of awkwardness that will end the evening and quite possibly the relationship that you inserted yourself into.

Moreways.

Whether you're playing with four, five, six, seven, or more, the rules are relatively the same. Be sure to have a Director to help the groups and duos move effortlessly between each other, or just throw caution to the wind and see what ends up happening. In this sort of a situation it's less important that there may be a member or two that you don't prefer. If there are enough bodies in the room, you can avoid one guy or another without any feelings being too hurt.

Sex parties.

For a second I was concerned about tackling this subject. Mainly because I don't want to get all the guff for the "downfall of gay rights" because men like to be in a room with a ton of other men fucking. But you know what? High school girls have blow job parties and swinger parties are still very much a thing in the hetero world. So here I go.

There are different kinds of sex parties. There are back rooms (dark areas) at underwear parties that turn into all-out orgies. These are usually very dark. If you decide to enter into one of these rooms, try not to be too picky about who you let touch you. You are entering into a pitch black space full of guys with mere millimeters between them. If you want to choose who you do what with, this is not the place for you. Also I'll say it again: be safe. Carry condoms with you tucked into your waistband.

A tiny packet of lube would be wise too. You are in a high-risk situation here. Be aware.

There are also more for-profit sex parties. These are held at clubs in certain countries, states, and in private residences and businesses in other cities. These types of events charge a cover and often have a guy at the door who checks out your body before you are granted entrance. As odd as this suggestion might seem, I think it's very smart to bring someone with you. Whether it's a friend you don't mind seeing naked or a friend whom you've slept with before, it's good to be with someone you trust who can help to get you out of a jam. A lot of these types of events also have a mandatory condom policy. Even if they don't, put one on.

You can always throw your own sex party too. If you go that route, be prepared for damage to your home whether in the form of stains on carpets or condoms all over the place. I suggest having liquor available and a soundtrack playing. Be very careful about who you invite, don't let any strangers get ahold of your address, and try not to invite two people who hate each other. Since you're the host, you make the rules. Tell them to respect your place and then try to have as much fun as possible.

Face Your Fetishes

Gay men have sex. It's just something we do, but how we have our sex is as varied and different as can be. Some guys are vanilla. Some guys dig feet. Some keep their socks on. Some like to role play. Some are into leather and/or bondage. Some only do it with more than one guy at a time. You know what? That's awesome. One of the most important outcomes of sex is pleasure and why shouldn't you get all the pleasure you can out of it?

Do you have a fetish? Chances are you do. Everyone does. If you don't think you do, perhaps you haven't discovered it yet. You'll know when you do. One day a guy will ask you to lick his sweaty armpit and you'll think "Ew, that's gross. That's weird." Then you'll do it and you'll think "Oh my God that's weirdly hot. Oh my God! I wanna do it again." Suddenly you'll be licking every bed mate's armpits. Congratulations, you have discovered that you have an armpit fetish! Go forth and lick every musky pit you find in your travels!

Never deny your fetishes. I know way too many guys who have a kink that they do not engage in because they are afraid of turning off or scaring or weirding out a guy they are with. What this ultimately leads to is uninspiring and less-exciting sex than they could actually be having. If there's something that drives you wild, you should certainly embrace it. Vanilla sex is a fantastic thing, but why not throw some sprinkles on it and really enjoy yourself?

The worst thing that can happen is that the guy you're with isn't into it and he will tell you so. More often though you'll discover that your partner might be willing to try out whatever you want to do. Even better than that, the odds are in your favor that your partner might end up digging it too!

For the sake of repetition everyone has a fetish or two. You might have an underwear fetish. Maybe you're into getting tickled. Maybe you just want your partner to slap you a few times and choke you a little bit while he does his thing. Maybe you want to be called a dirty whore while you're going at it. Maybe you're interested in trying water sports on for size. Maybe you have a thing for getting your nipples pinched and wrenched. Whatever it is you're fully entitled to your own kinks and fetishes.

If you find yourself in a sexual scenario where you don't think your kink or fetish is welcome, it's fine to not pursue it. But if you end up going further with this particular guy and seeing him more regularly, I really do hope that you consider letting him in on your dirty little interests. Otherwise you'll be doomed to having sex that doesn't give you everything that you want. That won't be fun. You won't enjoy it.

Conversely if you find yourself with a guy who springs his fetish on you, I recommend you give it a try unless it's something you are truly not-at-all into. If that's the case, feel free to tell your partner that you're not really into that sort of thing and continue with your fun. However, if you're ambivalent or have no opinion on the proposal you've received, give it a whirl! Fetishes and kinks are a lot like Pokémon; you never know when you'll come across an amazing one in your adventures.

Collect them all, boys. We can trade them later for fun.

The Book of Partying

Finding the Balance

As a gay nightlife promoter it is obviously in my best interest that thousands of guys come out to my events, stay all night, and buy plenty of cocktails at the bar. That's how I pay my bills and buy my boyfriend nice things. So please come out and buy drinks and shots and pay the cover and help support my life!

I am a big believer in living a balanced life: working hard and playing hard. Problem is that there is a subset of individuals who party just a bit too hard (regardless of how hard they work during the day).

I am not here to tell you just how much you should drink and party. Each and every one of us has a different body and different internal workings. What might be too little sleep or too much alcohol for one man might be nothing to another. What I am here to do is advise you to keep an eye on yourself and your personal health. It also helps to listen to friends if and when they tell you that you might be going over the edge.

Life is tough. We all have earned the right to let our hair down, get a little tipsy, and party the night away. Like anything else in this world the importance of partying lies in intelligent moderation. One night out until 5:00 A.M. when you have work at 9:00 A.M. might be a wild one-time memory, but it's probably not the best idea to go for an entire party weekend without your head seeing a pillow.

We are not immortal. We are not impervious. While we may not see the negative effects of our current actions, the effects exist. Be careful with how, when, and how often you let loose. I want you to have all the fun you can, but I don't want you to have to pay the price for it later.

If you or someone you know might have a problem, there are programs that exist to help. Alcoholics Anonymous has been an amazing support system for many guys I've known to be heading down a treacherous road. For those with harder more illegal problems, Narcotics Anonymous support groups are likewise helpful. There is no shame in being sober or going to meetings. Every person I know to have gone into those supportive groups has come back out a stronger, smarter, and more successful person.

So party on boys… just not too hard.

Doing Drugs

Many people find it hard to believe that I am drug free, but that is the God's honest truth. I have my own reasons, mostly that I already have a very addictive personality and that nightlife is a tough enough industry to succeed in as it is. I don't need any chemical handicaps. My stance doesn't change the fact that drugs are very much a part of the club and bar culture around the world.

Let's get this out first: I do not advocate the use of either heroin or crystal meth. They are nothing but Fast Passes to a world of suffering, pain, and death. Don't do them. If you know someone who does, do the best you can to find help for them and seek treatment. He'll thank you later.

Now onto the "Club Class" of drugs. Again, I don't do these, but I also don't feel right telling people not to do them. Clearly they are illegal substances, but when has legality ever stopped someone from doing anything? All I can say is the following statement: make sure you have control over what you choose to do versus letting what you do have control over you.

When you decide to do drugs, be sure you are educated on what exactly you are putting into your body. Know what to expect in terms of positive and negative side-effects. Know how long the effects will last. Know the proper dosage. Be aware of what drugs or substances can and cannot be mixed together. Know the guy or girl who gave you the substance in the first place. All of this is very important because messing up any of this information could very well result in at best, an expensive hospital trip and at worst, an early funeral.

Furthermore, be prepared for the fact that you may never actually know what is inside of the powder, tablet, or droplet you are consuming. The problem with drugs being illegal is that they are not federally regulated, which means that there's no one looking at how the stuff is being made.

Another important thing to remember is that you shouldn't go at it alone when you're using a party substance. Be sure to be with good friends that you trust just in case you go off the rails. They may be the ones who bring you to the ER or talk you down from a particularly nasty side effect.

In the end just know that you are putting your body at risk for a potentially elevated suite of feelings. Is this worth the risk? That's up to you.

6 Ways to NOT Be A Drunken Mess

You've seen them. I've seen them. Hell let's be honest, you and I have probably been them at one time or another. I'm talking specifically about That Hot Mess at the party. Standing straight up is impossible so he's pitching back and forth as his head falls like it's suddenly filled with billiard balls. God forbid he should try to walk... FACEPLANT! Chances are this is the same guy who will soon have his ass kicked out of the club. Don't worry, he won't go far. You'll find him puking on the sidewalk and crying right around the corner.

Can we please agree that this is not fun? Of course becoming intoxicated is fun. Getting drunk is fun, but the fun stops when you hit this point. When everything you drank is all over your shirt along with that slice of pizza, the fun has officially come to a stop.

Why do people get this way? Are they doing it on purpose? Are they so oblivious to their own personal limits? I have no answer. What I do have are some strategies that you can pass on to them, or use them yourself.

I am very well-versed in responsible liquor consumption for one reason: I refuse to allow myself to get extremely drunk at parties. I'll get tipsy and play it up, but that's where I stop. A good promoter can't be shit faced. He has to be ready to deal with problems, run the microphone, head up contests and giveaways, deal with issues at the door, meet and network, herd performers and go-gos, and attend to VIPs. Because of that I have developed a few guidelines that border on both science and art.

Unless you like waking up the next morning with puke still in your nostrils and no idea who that guy is in bed next to you, perhaps you'll take them to heart and give them a shot too!

Allow me to reiterate the following: I'm not saying you should be sober. Fuck no. Drink up! What I am advocating for here is a tiny bit of responsibility. I'm advocating knowing when to stop so we don't have to stop you by throwing your ass out on the street.

Here we go.

1. **Eat something.** Gays don't eat! Gays don't eat! Shut the fuck up. You need to eat something, preferably before you party. A few pieces of low-calorie bread if you're afraid of that upcoming photo shoot you have scheduled. What you need is carbs and protein. Just pretend you're building a small pillow or sponge in your tummy that will sop up the booze. An empty stomach is a dangerous thing when you're drinking because it could very well jump you from sober to trashed in just a drink or two.

2. **H20 breaks.** When I drink I play a game of tennis. The game is played in the following way: alcohol, bottle of water, alcohol, bottle of water, alcohol, bottle of water, bottle of water, alcohol. A bartender once told me: "Getting drunk is a funny thing. You're basically dehydrating and poisoning yourself." BRING IT ON! Let's drink. Seriously though, you need to rehydrate as you dehydrate. Imagine every cocktail drawing water out of your body. That's water you need to put back in there. As an added bonus hydrating may help you fight off a hangover!

3. **Secret ninja shots.** I very, very rarely take shots. Why? Because it's basically like guzzling an entire drink in one breath. Not good. It jumps you to hot mess a lot quicker. And yet as a promoter, I am constantly being pulled into shot scenarios where someone is buying and I better be drinking. So what do I do? I simply pour my shot into my drink. BOOM! You can pretend you're doing the shot and no one calls you out on it. You still get the booze so your free liquor opportunity isn't ruined and chances are it won't ruin the taste of your drink either.

4. **Space it out.** Listen, I know you're afraid we're going to run out of alcohol. Do not worry. We are fine. We have tons of bottles under the bar and even more in storage. You don't need to keep slamming them back with such abandon. Try spacing out your drink orders. Don't order a new drink until thirty or so minutes after your last one, or twenty minutes, or whatever.

5. **Make one night a science project.** This isn't going to be fun… but it's really helpful. Choose one night sometime soon and make it your "Study Night." What you're going to do is monitor yourself as closely as you can throughout the night. You want to be conscious of your level of intoxication as you drink. This will be tough because as the drinks go down things will start to go blurry. So drink slow. Do your waters. While doing this keep asking yourself "How drunk am I?" This will help you to determine your limit.

Thanks to a night like this I know the following: Two and a half drinks get me tipsy. I can have another drink every forty five minutes after this and maintain my tipsiness all night. Somewhere between three and four drinks without that pacing gets me drunk. Five drinks or more is too much for me. For every person it's different and it differs also based on the amount of sleep you've had, how hydrated you are, and if you ate anything that day. Even the temperature outside affects you. There are many different factors. Take a night and learn your body. It will thank you later for taking the time.

6. **Be happy with drunk.** Work with me people. You need to figure out when your happy drunk ends and when horror arrives. Do you need to take yourself to, or near, that regrettable point, or can you have an amazing night when you're tipsy? For me all I need is a little lightness in my head. I know that the second things start going crooked that the fun stops there. I know that if I can't walk without the world whirling around then I'm no longer having fun. I also know that if I get drunk enough I'll have to deal with the spins when I get home and try to go to sleep. There is nothing worse than that. Find the point that you need to reach to have the most fun and stick with it! There is no need to keep drinking. You can always have more the next morning at brunch.

"Whoa," you're thinking. Is a nightlife promoter telling me to maybe drink less? Sorta, and not in a judgmental way at all. As a promoter all I want is for everyone to have fun. No one's having fun if he is also having to hold his own puke in his hands.

We can get drunk and crazy and avoid all of that… so let's avoid it shall we?

It's Never Too Late to Irish Exit

One of the greatest skills you can master in the world of nightlife is the "Irish Exit." Also sometimes called "Ghosting," this is the process of leaving a bar, club, or party without telling anyone that you are leaving. Irish Exiting is a very simple act: just head towards the exit, go through it, and head home.

I am a master of the Irish Exit and I don't feel bad about it. Sure if you went to a house party, it might be considered rude to leave without giving your good-byes to all in attendance. This is not the case when you are out and about town. Chances are that you know many of the people there and you'll be seeing most of them really soon. Chances are that they won't even realize you've gone considering how far gone they are. So go ahead and head home before the next round of drinks or shots hit the bar. Your body will thank you for the extra rest and relaxation and the slightly lower alcohol intake.

Irish Exiting is a fantastic strategy if you discover you've had too much. If you still have some sense swimming around in your head with all of the tequila, make your exit before it's too late. It'll help prevent you from becoming "that guy" who's puking all over the place or making a total ass of himself. No one wants to make a scene. But if your boys are going hard all night, an Irish Exit may be your only course of action. Friends are great to have, but they're also really good at pushing us to do things we may regret later. If you feel like you've had one too many, ghost the hell out of there and grab a bottle of water on your way home.

Also, if you've been following a guy around or trying to get him to take interest in you and you just aren't feeling a response, an Irish Exit is a perfect move. It's better to leave too early versus too late. It might pique his interest in you at best. At worst it'll stop you from making an ass of yourself chasing after tail that has no interest in you.

Irish Exiting isn't always what the doctor ordered. If you came out in a duo or tight-knit group of friends, your ghosting could cause concern, worry, and confusion. In this case a "Partial Irish" is okay. Tell your immediately important friends that you have to leave and then be gone. If you're afraid that they may pressure you into staying or drinking more, you can also ghost and text them immediately after you've put a safe enough distance between you.

Party Pack Mentality

So you're going out tonight. Who's coming along? The number of people you decide to go out with can fundamentally change how your night will progress and the type of fun that you will have. There is no right number of people to go out with as each has its own unique positives and negatives. Let's take a look at them.

Going solo.

This is my preferred method of going out, but it works for me. Since I work in nightlife here in New York City, I know that there will be many of my friends out wherever I go. Whether they're at the party or working the party there will be familiar faces. If you know that there will be a number of guys you know when you go out, I suggest you consider the solo option as well. This allows you to fully embrace your social butterfly. You arrive when you want to arrive and you exit when you want to exit. Furthermore, you are free to flit around the bar or club and chat with anyone you want. You are beholden to nobody and nobody is beholden to you. Want to go to another bar? Go ahead! Want to go hit on that guy? Go for it! Want to link up with those friends you saw on the dance floor? You're the boss!

Granted not all is rosy with this option either. You don't have a wingman if you want to approach a guy. You won't necessarily have someone to talk to the second you arrive at the club.

There's also a certain fun that only occurs when you share your full night with other friends. I personally don't mind standing at the bar by my lonesome and challenging myself to approach people to get to know them. If you're not much of a loner, I recommend against this. Most importantly if you're a drug user or a disastrously heavy drinker, I do not at all recommend this option. You should never get plastered, blasted, or high without someone there just in case something goes awry. Nothing's more horrifying than being dragged into an ambulance or police car by strangers with no one around to calm you down.

You plus one.

You can always grab a bestie and head out for the night. Many people do this. The benefits of this is that, well you're not alone for one. You have a travel buddy for the cab or car or train. If you get approached by someone you don't like, your bestie can always pretend to be your boyfriend. You also have someone looking out for you to stop you from doing something dumb when you're stupid drunk.

The negatives of this option must also be weighed out. For one, if you meet a guy, are you sure your friend will be okay with you ditching him? Many friends are, but make sure before you go out that this is discussed lest you create a problem where there wasn't one before. Also if your friend gets really wasted, you have basically volunteered to be his babysitter and nurse. You might end up holding his hair back as he pukes or riding in an ambulance with him to the ER if something more serious happens.

You plus crew.

Did you love Mean Girls? Do you have your own version of the Plastics? Many gay guys answer "Yes!" Whether you're a gang of four, a caravan of seven, or a gaggle of thirteen, there's something very comforting about going out with your own tight-knit crew in tow. The first plus is that because there are so many of you it's a little easier to separate if and when it is called for. Someone found a guy? Off he goes! The remaining crew is still plenty dynamic enough to keep the night going. There's also strength in numbers. Your gang can approach a few guys, engage them, and basically swallow them like some sort of amoeba. Also when there's a bunch of you each has a unique offering to the night: someone is the talker, someone is the guy who buys everyone drinks when he's drunk, someone is really good at talking someone else down from a bad high.

Be warned there are also downfalls to the crew outing. For one, all of those people and egos means that problems may arise within your crew. Are two of the guys fucking? Did they get wasted and now they are fucking? Maybe two of them like the same guy. Maybe four of them want the same guy and that guy is you. Complications can very easily arise when you're all moving around in a massive group. Prepare for them. A crew is also a lot harder to move around. It's sort of like a Tyrannosaurus with a tiny brain located very, very far from its limbs. Good luck getting all of you together at one time and getting somewhere when you planned on it. Also, members will go missing throughout the night and now you all must go on a hunt to find whomever disappeared. I've seen crews take an hour to find one-another and then another thirty minutes just to move to the next bar a block away. This is why I never travel with a crew. But, maybe it's the right option for you. That's cool. You do you.

The Top 10 Things NOT To Do at The Gay Club

Since I spend most of my time in the bars and clubs of NYC I've been able to come up with this list of the Ten No-No Commandments. These are the things you do not do when out and about on the party scene. They may seem dumb to you... but you'd be surprised how often they happen.

1. **Do not fight with the doorman or bouncer.** He will kick your ass out of there. He will ban your ass from the bar. He will not let you go get your shit from coat check. They are here to maintain order. They may be gruff or tough, but that's their job. Your job is to make their job easier.

2. **Do not give a go-go boy your phone number.** This is his job and you're not as slick as you think you are. Smile, say "Hi," and give him a fucking tip so he can pay his utilities bills on time.

3. **Do not ask the host/promoter/anyone to get you in without an ID.** While we promoters like to act like we're "All That," the truth is we have our limits. One of these limits includes getting you and your underage friends into the bar. The bar doesn't want to close down or lose its liquor license. We don't want to lose our jobs. So drink a Four Loko at home and jerk off while you count down to your 21st birthday.

4. **Do not wash off your hand X's if you're under 21.** You're at an 18+ party and it's just so easy to age three years! Just wipe the X's off your hands and presto-change-o! You're legal! No, you're not. Any bar worth its muster has at least twenty-five to fifty video cameras that just caught you breaking the law.

5. **Do not deal or do drugs.** This is so terribly illegal. Do you want to go to jail? Another tidbit of information that's fun to know is that drug trafficking and sales at a club literally threaten the venue. If cops discover a bar or club is a hotbed of the toxic letters of the alphabet they will levy fines and even shut the place down. Do you want to shut down your favorite bar or club? I sure hope not.

6. **Do not have sex in the bathrooms.** Those stalls are filthy with a capital Holy Fuck These Things Are Nasty. Do you really want to pull out your pole in a place like that? Want to get on your knees in a puddle of God knows what? It's not even about having class. It's about not getting piss and puke on your jeans. It's about not licking the metal of the urinal by mistake.

7. **Don't give the DJ song requests.** This isn't a completely hard and fast rule. Taking requests is a pleasure or a pain depending on which DJ is spinning at the time. If the DJ wants to take your requests, he will make it absolutely known. He'll tell the crowd to come up or text him or hold up one of those phone apps that scroll words on them. In that case request away! Remember to be respectful to your fellow party-goers. Don't request some horrible, slow song that would never fly at a club. Think before you ask. If the DJ doesn't say he wants requests, he probably doesn't want them. Don't come up to his booth and interrupt him. Let him do the thing that he was paid to do.

8. **Do not start a fight.** We will kick you out. Most likely for quite a few months after the offense. Nightlife is for fun not for fighting. Take your shit outside and around the block. Learn to channel and dilute your anger and have another cocktail.

9. **Do not be an attention whore.** No one likes a whore. (Okay, maybe some GOP politicians). Absolutely no one likes an attention whore. Do not become one by avoiding the following: shrieking, dancing so others stare, bragging about your friend the bartender, acting like you're better than everyone else, screaming "THIS IS MY JAM," and genuinely acting like you're the hottest guy in the room. These actions tend to automatically render you the least hot guy in the room. Eyes will roll. You will be ignored. Have a good time and get your head out of your ass. No one likes a braggart.

10. **Do not arrive on gay time.** If a guest list ends at 12:00 A.M., be there by 11:30 P.M. If an open bar lasts an hour, get there twenty minutes before it starts. Arriving on time is arriving late and arriving late is arriving way too late. Plus the later you get to a party, the longer the line will be. This is because everyone gets there late. Don't think you can cut the line, because you won't be able to. Then you get to stand outside and whine about it while everyone else has fun. Nightlife waits for no gay with a busted watch. So get your ass to the club on time. Whatever you're doing can be done tomorrow, at the club, or not at all.

The Book of Living

Come Out, Come Out

The world is changing. Once upon a time gay men had to hide who they were from society. Being gay was a punishable crime. It was a mental disorder for which quack doctors recommended everything from imprisonment and drugs to electro-shock therapy. This wasn't even all that long ago. Men would wear bandanas around their arms to identify their sexuality and their kinks. They fucked in the dark recesses between buildings and on the docks and in the shadows.

Nowadays, you can't change the channel on your TV without coming across a gay character. You may not like how that character is portrayed, but there he is being gay and showing the millions of viewers that gays are a real thing. Every day more and more gays are coming out of the closet and proudly saying who they are and who they love.

I am not ignorant. I am fully aware that there are many places in our country where coming out and being proudly gay is not easy. It is still legal (as of me writing this) for employers to fire people for their gender identity or preference. It's mind boggling to imagine this as I write at my desk in my Hell's Kitchen apartment watching happy gay couples walk by holding hands. It is hard to believe but true.

But look where we've come from. At least what we're doing can't land us in jail any longer. At least we can't be committed to a psych ward because we choose to love someone we love. Every other day I see a news item about how a federal judge has struck down yet another gay marriage ban in another ass-backwards state that was too ignorant to do away with the law themselves. We are getting somewhere.

What does that have to do with your coming out process? Tragically it doesn't matter at all. While the world you live in may be making leaps and bounds in acceptance, this may not reflect personal surroundings. You may come from a very religious family. You may live in a backwards town or city or state where being who you are could be a very dangerous path to tread.

I am not going to be that guy who says that everyone must absolutely come out to everyone they know or see or meet right now. I will not tell you that it will advance our cause. Our cause is advancing one step at a time with those who were able to come out and start fighting. If you don't feel that coming out is a safe and smart bet for yourself, please don't rush it.

There is something else you should consider: You do not need to come out to everybody even once you're out. For example, my grandfather does not know that I am gay. He is literally the only member of my family who's unaware of my sexuality. I've had a few people say "How can you be okay with your grandfather not knowing who you really are?" I've told those people to shut up. My Gramps loves me unconditionally. He's always been my biggest cheerleader in business and life. He knows I'm working on this book. He just doesn't know what it's about. He knows I throw large, successful dance parties in New York City. He just doesn't know that they're gay parties. My grandfather was born in a different time in a different world. He's pushing ninety years old. I don't feel any sort of need to come out to him and force him to deal with that. He loves me as a person and is proud of me and cares about me. The fact that he doesn't know that I am gay doesn't make me feel like he loves or knows me any less. I am okay with him not knowing. Feel free to act similarly boys. Not everyone needs to know. Especially those who you know will never understand.

Your sexuality is yours as is your struggle to gain acceptance for it. Just like I'm not going to get into a debate with a Fox News viewer about anything because I know that my words will fall on deaf ears, you don't need to tell someone you are gay and then try to move them to accept you for it. They won't accept you? That's fine. Your time is better spent with people who will learn to accept you and will champion and support you.

Do Something

Hey! Hey you! What the fuck are you doing? That's the question I want to ask each and every single one of you today. Let me repeat it nice and clearly: "WHAT THE FUCK ARE YOU DOING?"

Think this through. I don't mean "I'm having lunch, JL." or "I'm at my day job, JL." That's fine. No I mean something deeper and more meaningful. So let me get more specific. What the fuck are you doing that you don't have to be doing?

I have found that a lot of people I meet do very little outside of what they have to do. They do the day job thang. They do the workout thang. They do the eatin, peein, poopin, and sleepin thang. And then…? The TV thang? The video game thang?

That's fine, but I am here to challenge you to do more than that. As my grandpa still says to this day, do more than what is expected of you. This applies to life. Each and every one of you reading this has a passion. You must. You have to. It's written into your DNA. It's in your very genetic code. Whether that passion be technology, music, art, whatever.

Are you spending time every day indulging in your passion? Are you writing a song? Sketching out a comic book? Writing a play? If not, what the fuck are you doing? I'll tell you what you're doing: you're wasting time. I'm not saying stop going out. I'm not saying quit your day job. I'm saying you should invest at least thirty minutes a day creating.

In my opinion, the meaning of life is creation. We are here to create and to share what we create. Every day I create. Because I feel empty, pointless, useless, and lonely if I don't create. I also have enough irons in the fire that I can create something different every day.

What about you? Are you creating? If so, keep on doing it. If not, it's time to get started. You can only enjoy life so much by eating, drinking, dancing, and watching TV. You like watching TV a lot? Start a web series. It's astoundingly affordable. You like playing video games? Get together with a bunch of your nerd friends and try making one.

This isn't about making money (though I do believe that when you work long, hard hours and continuously on something you actually love and enjoy, you're almost guaranteed success in it). It's about making. Period. And no excuses...

"I would, but I don't have the time!"

Sure you do. You're reading this right now. You could be doing that instead. I'll bet if I followed you around for a day I could identify at least an hour's worth of time that you unconsciously squander.

"I would, but I don't have the money!"

Thanks to the Internet basically everything is free or astoundingly cheap these days. Don't have enough money? Do a Kickstarter (I did! It worked! Thanks to all of you who helped with that, btw.) If you're creative enough, you'll find that whatever you want to do can be done for nothing or for very cheap.

"I would, but I have to plan it first!"

No! There shall be no planning. Planning is nothing but an excuse to not do something. Plan while in progress. Start doing something and figure it out as you go along. Do you know how many novelists I know who have been "working on" a book for years? Right. I wrote my first novel in thirty days and edited it over nine months. I wrote the second one in the following three months. Then two more short stories. And now this. Get to work!

"I would, but I'm not passionate about anything!"

Take a closer look at yourself friend. You have a passion. Figure it out. Think around it and if you have a bunch, try 'em all on for size! There are no rules here because you're in charge because you're creating it. Fuck everyone else. This is about you enjoying yourself and making something where there was once nothing. Whether it's a recipe website, a new type of sock, or a monologue.

"But I'm going to do this thing, so I can make money and be successful."

This is a big mistake. You need to love the thing you're doing. That way when it's not an immediate success, you don't give a shit because you love doing it any way.

Make something. Do something. Next time you see me out at the clubs or on the street or in an IM box on Facebook I'm going to ask you what the fuck you are doing. You better have an answer.

Work Hard, Dream Hard

When I meet new people I often ask them what it is that they do. More often than not, they tell me their profession while simultaneously rolling their eyes and sighing very sadly. I then follow up by asking them what it is that they'd rather be doing. Oh they love that question. They want to be a dancer, or a cartoonist, or a stand-up comedian, or whatever.

There is nothing wrong with doing a job that you don't want to be doing. My stepfather has a habit of saying "They wouldn't call it work if you enjoyed it." This is true to a degree. If you need to work to pay your bills and live your life, then work you must. If you don't need to work, I hate you but I'll get over it. The rest of us need to earn a weekly paycheck if we want to keep the electricity and water running in our homes. Thus we work.

If the job you're currently doing isn't what you want to be doing, you better be doing something about it. I spent the first decade of my adulthood (post-college) working in public relations and advertising. I thought I loved it. I thought it was everything I'd ever want to do. Then one day I tripped and fell into the world of gay nightlife and discovered that I had spent the past seven years of my grown-up life climbing a ladder that I suddenly wanted to get off of.

There is a subset of people you will see on reality competitions and occasionally meet in real life who quit their jobs, move into their cars, and fully pursue their passions. I guess that's fine. It's way too risky for me and I certainly cannot recommend it.

Blame my mother who did a great job of putting the fear of going broke and being homeless in me at a very young age. So what did I do? I doubled down.

I continued working in my 9:00-5:00 day job (which at the time was more like an 8:00-8:00 day job) and started doing nightlife as well. I was also writing a novel at the time, so I did that too. I would come home from work, plop down at my computer, and write for an hour. When that was done I showered, dressed, and headed out to the club. My free time became my passion time. My video games and TV and social life outside of club scenarios where I was being paid to attend took a backseat. A sacrifice? Absolutely. In fact I might argue it's a larger sacrifice than quitting your job and going all-in.

After three years of this harrowing triple-dipping, I finally reached a point where my nightlife and day life were both making excellent money. This was when I made the final sacrifice. I could keep both jobs and the ridiculous double-salary I was earning, or I could chop it in half and take the dive. I chose the latter option. Today I work from home without wearing pants, go out to parties and clubs every night of the week, and don't wake up until noon. I am very content. I am working even harder in my new life (nightlife is very much a 24-7 on-call type of job) but I love every minute of it.

My work is exhausting but rewarding. I love what I'm doing and the fun is almost never-ending. It makes the three years of driving myself beyond the brink of exhaustion totally worth the outcome.

If you feel stuck in your job, just remember you're not stuck. Start using your free time to work on your dream job. You'll be sleep-deprived and grumpy and quite possibly psychotic, but it is the only way to go about it in my book. Double down. Work hard at your job and then work hard when you get home. Don't expect the magic to happen right away. If you love what you're doing during your free time, it won't feel like work anyway.

Play For Karma

This isn't a spiritual book, so I won't spend too long defining karma for you. Plus, I think that most people kind of know what it is. It is a Buddhist concept that when we put energy out into the universe it comes back to us threefold. If you do something evil, you're screwed. If you do something good, hooray!

Whether karma is a real thing or not, I live my life as though it is. It's the Google motto of "Don't be evil."

Every day I try to do one good deed. You should do the same. Doing something good for someone and seeing their happiness is an amazing reward in and of itself. Surprising a boyfriend or friend or family member with a gift, or giving that homeless person a dollar, or going out of your way to help a friend move are all good deeds as far as I'm concerned.

Try it out! If you're doing it already, keep it up. If you aren't, give it a shot.

Even if you can't pull off one good deed a day do take the time to make sure that you aren't doing one bad thing a day. Catch yourself before you screw someone over, or speak ill of someone, or steal someone's cab, or insult or make fun of a complete stranger. This sort of behavior is poisonous and contagious. The biggest problem is that sometimes it feels good. Don't fall into the habit of this sort of behavior. It will come back to bite you in the ass. And if karma is a real thing, you're really going to hate it when it triples and comes flying back at your head.

Avoid Unnecessary Conflict

I have learned that there are a few things I can never post about on Facebook without inciting a full on flame war. Some of the explosive subjects include Britney Spears, Lady Gaga, basically any diva, any RuPaul's Drag Race contestant or winner, and a ton of other things. As soon as my post comes up, out come the Stans and the Haters, their guns and torches at the ready for battle.

What a waste of time.

Everyone already has enough real conflict in life. Let's chill it out with the unnecessary battles that we engage in just because we're bored or getting ready to go out. Britney Spears doesn't need you to defend her honor and Lady Gaga will probably never know that you had something nasty to say about her.

I often feel this way about politics too. I am a bleeding heart, out-loud-and-proud Democrat. I will on occasion (when incensed) post something very strongly worded on my Facebook about some bullshit some GOP blowhard said or did. And then out come my Republican friends to take me on. The point is I don't engage them. Maybe back in the day of Public Houses where there was no TV, or radio, or Internet, or phones this sort of debate was necessary. Nowadays it's just wasted time.

I know that I am not going to change these Republicans' opinions. I know that fighting with them is like getting into an argument with a fire hydrant. Nothing will change besides how much time I've wasted accomplishing absolutely nothing. So I state my opinion, and then I step away.

Consider doing the same. Spare yourself the anger and volatility of going at someone to try and change their mind about someone who will never see your exchange.

In the end remember that everyone is entitled to their own opinion. If you disagree, remember that whether they're entitled or not you won't be changing their mind any time soon.

Five Ways to Avoid Drama

Once upon a time it was something the gays and the losers (and me) did when they were in high school since they weren't cool or strong enough to participate in sports. Nowadays it's something that most gay men would say infects and lords over each and every one of our lives with an iron fist (which is forever clutching a Cosmo magazine).

It seems almost inevitable: drama is like a really loud annoying friend. Perhaps the member of Bad Girls Club who got kicked off the show early because she lit someone's weave on fire. You cannot avoid the queen. Wherever you go there she will be, screaming and pulling her earrings out and slathering Vaseline on her face as she comes after you with her press-on nails bared and twinkling in the club lighting.

Is drama actually avoidable? I'm going to go ahead and state this confidently: you can be drama free.

Below you will find just a few tips to avoiding drama. This is assuming you want to avoid drama. It is an undeniable fact that it feels good to join in a bitch session about some ex or slut or loser. It inflames the pleasure centers of our brains. Until it's turned around on us, then it sucks. So if you love drama, read no further. If you'd like to surgically remove some of it from your day-to-day, continue reading!

1. You know nothing. I'm sure this isn't exactly true. In fact there's a very good chance you know a lot. You know who's cheating on who. You know who said who's got an ass wider than the Lincoln Tunnel after a bomb went off in it. Hell, you may be the guy that everyone tells everything to. (I'm one of these people). But guess what? I'm going to say this slowly: You. Know. Nothing.

When someone says "Did you hear (blah drama drama blah)?" Your answer needs to be a facial response that borders on brain-dead and a shrug of your shoulders followed by "Duh... what are you talkin' about chief?" You have just stopped potential future drama in its tracks. A nice side effect comes of this: everyone will trust you. You earned it. You are a fabulous lock box... or a random hole in the woods into which everyone can chuck their filthy laundry with no fear of it being puked back onto them at a later date.

2. Trust no one. This is not a negative or hateful rule. It is just something you have to do. There are only two people I tell my secrets to: my mom and my brother. The reasons for this include neither of them understand what the fuck I am talking about and my brother is too busy being straight, hot, and a successful actor touring the country to care. If you must tell things to someone, make sure he (or she) is so divorced from the scene that he wouldn't know what to do with the information you are giving him, even if for some reason they wanted to.

I'm not advising against deep, trusting friendships/relationships with people. I'm not saying the solution to drama is to become a killer, emotionless robot. Rather I'm saying develop wonderful, deep relationships with people and use that love to support each other and spread happiness, instead of poisoning the well and bitching and moaning about others.

3. Know the math. The formula for drama is deceptively simple:

Person A tells Person B a secret or something negative about Person C.

Person B can do a few things from here to cause trouble. For one, they can tell a Person D. Person D can now start drama in one of two ways: One, he tells Person A and now Person B and Person A have drama because Person A told Person B a secret he trusted him with. DRAMA! RUN!

Even worse is Person D telling Person C. Now Person A has drama with Person C, and they both have drama with Person B. And Person D will probably hop on the Goodship Drama as well just because it's fun.

Another possible issue can be Person B going straight to Person C and telling them what Person A said, cutting Person D out of it entirely. (Which is fine. No one ever liked Person D any way, that shady cunt). This scenario is probably the most toxic and dangerous. You have a No-Love Triangle that will no doubt resolve itself with either a fist fight or someone ending up in the East River.

In the end if Person A said nothing, the formula would fail. If you're Person B and Person A has told you something about Person C, it is your responsibility to stop the drama right there. Otherwise, you could be in a lot of trouble.

Make your head spin? That's fine. Your head will spin a lot more when it's getting bitch-slapped from all angles by a bunch of angry gays. The solution to this formula? Rules 1 and 2. Keep your secrets and tell them to your stuffed animals or goldfish.

4. Throw your opinions away. The sneaky thing about drama is you can get caught up in it even if you don't tell someone else! If the Drama Spreader tells you something and you have a catty opinion about what they're telling you, you've just committed a response. Now the Drama Spreader can spread drama to others, and might very well add to his drama a comment involving you and how you thought that Kris was also a dirty bottom whore. Each one of those people the Drama Spreader spreads to may now rat out the Spreader, and you in tow for your seemingly private reaction.

The secret? Nod dumbly. Maybe you can say "Wow" or "Huh, that's wild." Do NOT have a negative (or positive) reaction. Having a neutral reaction guarantees that you can't be thrown under The Drama Bus.

5. Care about nothing. The biggest secret to avoiding drama is to not get caught up in the emotions of it all. In fact you can skip steps 1-4 if you can perfect this one.

Remember life is about having fun, living, and achieving your dreams. It's also about going to the bathroom and feeding yourself. If you can hear from someone how someone else insulted you and honestly not care… not because he's a big slut, or he's an asshole, or because he's ugly, or because you're richer than him, but not care because in other countries people don't have food and thousands are dying from natural disasters and warfare every week, congratulations are due because you won the final battle. If you can do that, congratulations are due because you won the final piece. By not being hurt or taken down by what others say about you no matter how true, false, vile, mean, or villainous, you will surely avoid all potential forms of drama. Drama only hits those who care.

I'm too busy having fun and trying to be a nice guy to get caught up in drama. I've been called my fair share of things by others that I've heard later. I'm out of shape. I'm an egomaniac. I'm lucky in life, love, and finances and deserve none of my success. I'm a piece of shit. I'm a liar and a slut. I've heard it all. Does it hurt? Sometimes it does. But you know what? I hold no ill will against anyone else. Because in the end, what does it all matter? We have bigger things in our lives and the world to worry about.

Money Really Matters

Money is a funny thing… just kidding. It's a very fucking serious thing. It would be awesome if everything were free or if we were rich. Some of us are, but then there's the rest of us.

Listen up! I'm all about being young and having fun, but I'm going to play Papa Justin for a few minutes and give you a few important tips. Let me think about your future so you don't have to.

Save, save, save.

My mother raised me with a continuous fear of being poor and homeless. This may have been slightly cruel, but it was also effective. I now have a very large saving account. It wasn't always that way. I've been aggressively saving money since I was in college. I saved a bit here and there and as my salary and income increased so did my savings.

Saving money is boring. I'll admit that. I'd much rather go out and buy video games. But you know what? There's a nice feeling that comes with a sense of security. If I lost my job, I have enough in my savings to live income-free for a year or more. That's assuming zero income, which I would never allow myself to live with.

You can't touch that.

How did I save all the money I've put away? I snuck it away from me behind my back. I set up a second bank account online. I programmed it to tip-toe into my checking account once a week and pull out a chunk of money. In the beginning it was $50 a week. Then it was $100 a week. Now it's $500 a week.

I then treated the account like it didn't exist. If my checking account was low leading up to my next paycheck, then I lived with it. I cut corners. The rule was simple: I am not allowed to touch my savings. Done. Try it. Even if you're having $10 deducted a week, it's still something. It's a start.

Smart credit.

A lot of people are in disgusting amounts of debt. That's terrible and I'm sorry they have to face it. For me, my debt is always controlled and intentional. Essentially, I only charge what I can pay. My credit card bills are always paid in full. In fact, thanks to digital checking I often pay down numbers on my credit card the second they appear.

The only time I charge for more than I can afford is when the credit card lets me. For example, my favorite credit card is my Best Buy one. When I make a multi-thousand dollar purchase it allows me to pay down the charge, interest free, for anywhere from eighteen to thirty-two months. The catch is that I actually pay it down. I look at the total months and the total charge, and divide it to see exactly how much I need to pay a month in order to avoid interest.

Listen boys, if you're bad with credit, stop buying shit. Interest is the biggest sucker of them all. You're paying money (and potentially lots of it) for absolutely nothing. Spare yourself. Pay with a debit card. Live according to your actual income.

$1,000 ain't enough.

Somewhere there's an article that I read that says an astounding majority of Americans would need to borrow, beg, or steal just to get $1,000 if they suddenly needed it for an emergency. This is bad. This is very, very bad. You never know where your life might lead you. So get that $1,000... but do not stop there. You should have at least $1,000 saved away in a bank account somewhere. Start now if you don't have it. And then just keep on going.

Go for deals.

Every city is full of open bars, cover-free parties, giveaways, and freebies. You just have to look for them. I never miss an open bar when I'm going out. If you don't have the cash to afford drinks at the bar, drink at home first and then have one at the bar. Again, it's nice to live lavishly, but it can lead to ruin.

It could happen to you.

Now I go the fear route like my mother did with me. You're not impervious. Go watch the documentary Maxed Out. Credit and debt is a serious fucking thing. You could end up forty and homeless (hard to imagine when you're twenty-one and living the life... but you should).

My father was once a very wealthy man. Then he and my mother got divorced and he went on a spending binge. Then he was bankrupt, living on food stamps and in government housing. I took him out to meals and cut him monthly checks to help. Looking at my Dad ten years ago I never expected this. But it's very real and a terrible way to live. I watched him trying to survive every day.

I don't mean to be a killjoy. But since I'm probably the oldest gay you know (or near-to-the-oldest) I feel this is my responsibility.

1. Open a savings account.
2. Deposit in it weekly.
3. Avoid debt.
4. Use debit.
5. Live like you earn, not like you wish.

Just do it for Papa Justin m'kay? Your credit score will thank me.

All in the Family

I lost my father to prostate cancer two years ago. I consider myself very lucky that I was able to hop a train to Long Island to meet up with my brother and stand over Dad's bedside the night before he passed away. He wasn't able to talk, and for most of the time he kept his eyes closed. At least it didn't look like he was suffering. My father wasn't a perfect man (nor is any man or woman) but he was a fantastic, generous, selfless guy. He had his flaws, and he had his fair share of issues. But that final night, I took his hand and he squeezed back. I told him I loved him and would miss him and that I forgave him for all the things he had done many years ago that I told him I would never forgive him for. I cried. I took a ten second video of him lying on the bed, just breathing. I still have that video, and I watch it sometimes just so I can remember.

I didn't tell you this story so you could feel sorry for me. I merely want to make sure that you cherish your family while you have them. My father passed when he had just hit his sixties, a very young age for a man to exit this mortal coil. I thank God that I was able to see him before it was too late.

Family is very important to me, and it should be to you as well. I speak to my mother on the phone every single day. My brother and I speak at least weekly while he's touring around the U. S. being a super-famous, successful actor. I call my grandfather and try to find the correct middle ground between yelling and whispering so that he can hear me through the receiver.

Cherish your family. Spend time with them when you can. Pick up the phone right now and give them a call to see how they're doing. Even if you've had your ups and downs (who hasn't?) trust me when I say that you don't want to ever have regrets when they are gone.

Judge Not

When I was younger I was full of judgment. I judged guys who did porn. I judged guys who did drugs. Hell, I judged my ex-boyfriend because he drank to the point of getting drunk. I wasted so much time judging that I didn't have much fun in my younger twenties.

It wasn't until I got into nightlife that I was forced to come face-to-face with my inner judge. He was a stuffy old dude with a powdered wig and lots of wrinkles and there was nothing that he approved of. I didn't like this guy. He was a killjoy and an asshole. He had to go. So I knocked him out, threw him in a sack, and chucked him into the Hudson River.

You would do well to do the same. Every day I see guys passing judgment on every type of person and thing. This person thinks that guy is a slut because he sleeps with a lot of guys. That guy is a slut because he takes his shirt off and posts photos of it on Facebook. That guy doesn't put out and so he's a cock tease. That drag queen's eyelashes are wonky.

Why must we draw lines in the sand and judge anyone who crosses them? So what if you don't have as much sex? So what if you wouldn't wear a bathing suit that small? Does it matter? No. Consider that a virgin might consider you a slut or a Harvard grad might consider you stupid. It's all relative. We can all judge one-another if we wanted to, but we should refrain. There's simply no good reason.

To have the audacity to judge someone you have to first believe that you are better than that person. No one should walk around with that sort of internal thinking. It's not a good way to live, and it's a terrible way to relate to people.

We as gay people are already being judged every day. We are judged by prejudiced heterosexuals. We are judged by Fox News Channel and the religious right. We are judged by strangers on the street. Why in God's name do we want to judge one-another in our community? Wouldn't things be so much better if we all got along and became a powerful entity that could stand up to those people who truly hate us?

Skip the judgment. I'm not saying it's an easy task. It took me a long time to kill off my judgment. Sometimes I feel it sneaking back and I have to scream and bang sticks together to scare it off. As long as everyone is living the best life they can and aren't hurting anyone while they do it, I'm fine with it. I may not understand what they do, who they do, where they do, or why they do, but that's none of my business. Live and let live.

Conclusion

And that's all I wrote boys. Did you like it? I hope you did. I would love to hear what you thought of The Gay Gospel. Please shoot me a message on my website at www.JustinLukeNYC.com. I promise I'll respond in a timely fashion!

In the end, if I had to leave you with a few final takeaways, it would be to go out and live your life. Do your best to do no evil or spread ill will. Don't do anything that will hurt you or others around you. Help others and allow yourselves to be helped.

Love and live and learn as you go. Never make a five-year plan. Throw shit at the wall every day to see what sticks.

Go with the flow and understand that no life is absolutely perfect or completely happy. We are all flawed beings just stumbling along trying to make sense of what happens in the world around us.

Good luck. You'll need it, but be sure to have fun as you go. I'll be here rooting you on.

Love,

Justin Luke

Afterword

By Billy Porter

Alright, listen up...

When Justin asked me to write this piece I was worried.

I thought to myself: "If I had the choice between going back to my twenties and being waterboarded... I would choose the latter."

You see, my twenties are a blur at best. I'm a product of the pre-"Will & Grace/Modern Family generation," which is basically a code word for the AIDS crisis. I know I'm bringing the room down a bit, but I gotta be real. I jumped out of the frying pan and directly into the blazing fire when I came out at fifteen years old in 1985 in Pittsburgh, PA, and was practically banished from my Pentecostal upbringing. Only to, in my new found abomination of a life, be faced with the concept that my "lifestyle" was the cause of all the world's problems including, but not limited to my imminent death, which was ultimately the punishment for my "choice" to be homosexual.

Gay men were dropping like flies on a daily basis and no one seemed to care except us. We nearly lost an entire generation of gay men who were supposed to teach us how to be, how to navigate and function in a society that hated us so. The atmosphere at that time in our history was so panicked and toxic that there was very little energy left to focus on the mundane, silly, gay boy shit that we were supposed to experience. We had to pull up! We were on the front lines! We were becoming activists! We were changing the world! If some of you young bucks questioned as you were watching "The Normal Heart" on HBO if the depiction of that time in our history was exaggerated, I'm here to tell you - NO!

Which leads me to this GAY GOSPEL business. . .

I truly picked up this book with every intention of reading the first twenty pages to get the tone of Justin's writing and then firing off some sort of witty, fabulous, gay-lloquial realness moment and get the fuck on with my day. I have things to do! Places to be! Boots to be KINKY!!!

But by page ten the tears were streaming down my face. By page twenty I was inconsolable. I didn't understand why at first and then it hit me - OMFG, this book is for me! This book is for all of us! This book is especially for our lost generation who never fully had the luxury of simplicity.

I realized reading this deftly concise, incredibly lean, yet amazingly practical handbook that I needed every word on every single page. I don't mean to reduce these pages to mere pragmatic fluff. It's quite the opposite. Justin has not only introduced the Gospel to "the children" with this work; I believe he's penned a Bible that will have long-standing truths that prepare, advise, and inspire generations of "ladies in waiting" for years to come. Thank you Justin for the shot to my heart. I needed it. And remember my little Divas in training. . .

Be the best version of yourselves that you can be... because nobody does that better than you.

And. . . SUCK a dick! Don't BE one!

WEEEEEEEERRRRRRRRRRKKKKKKK!!!

Special Thanks

Thanks to Mom, Ray, Jared, Boyfriend Joe, Alan, and all of my supportive friends who helped me to get all of this info out of my head and onto the page.

Thanks to Alexander Tsopanakis of AVisuals for the amazing cover.

Thanks to Colby Duhon for the flawless copy-editing.

Thanks to the crew at 52 Novels, as always, for expert formatting.

And last, but not least, my thanks go to the following spectacular people who supported me financially via my Kickstarter campaign to help make this Gospel a reality: Zee A. VanBaker, Anthony James, Bobby Anspach, Isaiah Negron, Nick Laird, Michael Graye, Naseer Francois Ashraf, Daniel Conroy, Nic Trudell, DJ DrewG (Drew Montalvo), Joseph Drobezko, Luke Camp, Tos Sass, Joe Roszak, David Michael Kananowitz, Scott Ginett, Joey Be, Troy Diggs, Will Pilson, Scott Massey, Laurel Crown Productions, Travis Xavier Carroll, Jeffrey Levin, Ricky Dunlop, Christi Peters Kirzner, Rob Browatzke, Dakota James Butler, Mark Ferreira, DJ Mick Hale, Anthony Visciotti, Adam Sophiella, Jeremy Reese, Bryan Clay, Andrew Brandt, Ryan Russ, Savas Abadsidis, Daniel Mehlinger, Jim Pagano, Adam Schweig, Adam Tekeoglu, Juni Odaglas, Gavin Juckette, Jason Moriarty, Nick Evers, and Jonathan Wang.

About the Author

Justin Luke Zirilli is the Co-Owner and President of the New York-Based gay nightlife events company, BoiParty™. Together with his business partner, Alan Picus, they throw the three largest weekly gay dance parties in New York City.

Justin is the author of the best-selling gay novel Gulliver Takes Manhattan released on May 1st, 2012 in paperback, eBook, and audiobook from Amazon Publishing. He's also the author of the best-selling sequel Gulliver Takes Five released in October of 2012. He has also published a number of shorter works of fiction.

He is the creator of Gorgeous, Gay and Twenty-Something, a private international Facebook group now comprised of over 8,000 members.

When not being a party monster and/or writing, Justin spends his time in Hell's Kitchen, New York, usually playing Playstation 4 and watching BBC programming with his boyfriend, Joe.

For more information about Justin and his various exploits visit www.JustinLukeNYC.com.

Made in the USA
Middletown, DE
01 December 2014